Reclaiming Life

Talking Stick 30

Reclaiming Life

Talking Stick 30

A publication of the
Jackpine Writers' Bloc, Inc.

www.thetalkingstick.com
www.jackpinewriters.com
Send correspondence to sharrick1@wcta.net or
Jackpine Writers' Bloc, Inc., 13320 149th Avenue,
Menahga, Minnesota 56464.

Managing Editors: Sharon Harris, Tarah L. Wolff
Copy Editors: Sharon Harris, Niomi Phillips, Marilyn Wolff, Tarah L. Wolff
Layout, Production, and Cover Design: Tarah L. Wolff
Editorial Board: Sharon Harris, Mike Lein, Ryan Neely, Deb Schlueter, Tarah L. Wolff
Judges: Laura L. Hansen, Elisa Korenne, Jeanne Cooney

Contents

Contents

Contents

Contents

Contents

Co-Editor's Note - Sharon Harris
Editor's Choice "Taps" p.83 by Jim Bohen

My favorite poem is "Taps" by Jim Bohen on page 83. In the past, hearing the music to "Taps" has always affected me. This poem has phrases that reflect the mood of that music. It is lovely and full of melancholy thoughts and visions, heavy with the burdens of life and the knowledge of death. "Knowing less and less of youth, more and more of other truths."

This poem can make you ache with desolation, feel all the mournful parts of life and the absolute certainty that death will meet us all somehow, somewhere. It shows a person's heart aching, accepting the sorrow and knowledge of death, facing full into it. It is saying a farewell to the day, moving into the dusk and the dark.

Generally, I am cheerful and upbeat and looking ahead to further adventures in life—but I can also feel this sad knowledge of life and its inevitable ending. This lovely poem is not only a sad farewell to life, it is perhaps also a reminder to all of us that we still do have roads to travel, places to go, things to do, in the time we have left.

Coming through a year of a pandemic has made us all less confident in the good, easy life we perhaps used to have. I hope we can all start reclaiming that life and enjoy the music of the words in the poems and stories in Talking Stick 30.

Co-Editor's Note - Tarah L. Wolff
Editor's Choice "Autumn 2020" p.160 Meridel Kahl

Like with all our past Talking Sticks, we can mark the times we all went through in its pages. This one is an echo of the odd, everyday reality we all faced together . . . six feet apart. We've proven to be resilient though, and, when people say they want things back to the way it was, I don't entirely agree with them.

I felt like I had ten days to make ten years of steps into the 21st century at my day job. I was thrilled to finally do it, but you may not have believed it from the amount of colorful language I used over those weeks, and the weeks and months of implementation to follow. Now complete though, there is no going back.

These times proved that, to many, the nine-to-five in-person job was not just entirely outdated but bordering on absurd. If it ain't broke don't fix it—was no longer an excuse. More flexible hours and the choice to work from home and be with our families is an awesome new reality for many.

With everything closed down, the world had to learn to find fulfillment at home again. Scott and I joke about nearly killing each other in quarantine, but we depend on each other now like we always should have. Oftentimes it totally sucked, but those months gave us a much healthier and more private relationship.

We were forced to deal with where we were lacking, what we had been putting off, distracting ourselves from, procrastinating on and trying to ignore, not just in us and in our own households, but in our country. Necessary growth can be ugly, but I hope we'll look back and remember 2020-21 for all the good changes that came out of it.

Poetry

First Place "Sunday Morning Samba" p.1. Jana A. Bouma lives in southern Minnesota and works as an advisor at a community college. Her poems have appeared in journals such as *Natural Bridge* and *Sow's Ear Poetry Review*, as a text within David Kassler's "A Choral Song Cycle," and on signposts next to city bike trails.

Second Place "Losing the Wobble," p.10 Mary Lou Brandvik

Honorable Mention

"Prairie Sky," p.33 Christopher Mueller

"Suncatchers," p.29 Anne Seltz

"Phone Call," p.138 Amy C. Rea

". . . to the World," p.80 Tim J. Brennan

"Angel Light," p.70 Joel Van Valin

"Things Owned by the Man Who Made Me," p.44 Dawn Loeffler

Poetry Judge Laura L. Hansen is the winner of the N.F.S.P.S. Stevens Poetry Manuscript Competition and a Midwest Book Award Finalist for her poetry collection, *Midnight River*. Her writing has appeared in regional publications such as *Talking Stick*, *Martin Lake Journal*, *Stone Gathering*, online at *The Heron Tree*, and in *Lake Country Journal Magazine*. Laura was given a Community Arts Leadership Award by the Five Wings Arts Council in 2016 and is also a three-time Five Wings Individual Artist Grantee. Her most recent work, *The Night Journey: Stories and Poems* published by River Place Press, explores the intersection of art, landscape and story.

www.riverpoethansen.com or www.laurahansenbooks.com

Creative Nonfiction
First Place "At Rest," p.2. Christina Joyce has degrees in journalism and public administration, works as a government communicator by day, and dabbles in creative nonfiction writing by night. Her most recent essays were published in *Talking Stick* and the *Saint Paul Almanac.*

Second Place "Five Young Men and Christmas 2020," p.11
Darrell J. Pederson

Honorable Mention
"Movie Money," p.139 Bernadette Hondl Thomasy
"People Say the Dumbest Things," p.123 Pam Whitfield

Creative Nonfiction (& Humor) Judge Elisa Korenne, a Yale Graduate and award-winning songwriter known for her original songs about oddballs in history, left New York City in 2006 to be an artist-in-residence in rural west central Minnesota. Since becoming a Minnesotan, Korenne has become known as a pioneering rural artist. She began her music career in 2001 after leaving her role at the international development nonprofit she co-founded, Geekcorps, an alternate Peacecorps for technology professionals building businesses in developing countries. Her debut book, *Hundred Miles to Nowhere: An Unlikely Love Story* was available June 2017.
www.elisakorenne.com

Fiction
First Place "Charlie and Ruby," p.4. Anne M. Jackson is the mother of two delightful hooligans and she is married to her favorite human. Her Labrador would tell you that her writing tastes delicious. Anne writes novels, short fiction, essays, and poetry.

Second Place "Hills of Iron," p.13 Kate Bitters

Honorable Mention
"Crevices," p.109 Marlys Guimaraes

Fiction Judge Jeanne Cooney. After a career with the U.S. Department of Justice, where she directed a communications division out of the U.S. Attorney's Office in Minneapolis, Jeanne moved back to northwestern Minnesota, where she now writes humorous mysteries. Her first three-book series was *The Hot Dish Heaven Mysteries with Recipes*. She's presently writing the second book in her next series. The first book in that series, *It's Murder, Dontcha Know?* is expected to be released nationally in April of 2022. She also does humorous public speaking at conferences and events, and she's an Artist in Residence for the Northwest Minnesota Regional Arts Council.
www.jeannecooney.com

Humor
First Place "Rats," *(Creative Nonfiction)* **p.8.** Tara Flaherty Guy has a BA in Creative Writing from Metropolitan State University in St. Paul, Minnesota, and works as a contributing writer at St. Paul Publishing Company. Her work has been published in *Yellow Arrow Journal*, *Talking Stick*, and *Adelaide Literary Magazine*, with her latest work forthcoming in *Miracle Monocle* and *The MacGuffin*.

Second Place "Cat on Fire," *(Fiction)* **p.16 Anne M. Jackson**

Honorable Mention
"Stupid Ramblings," p.97 *(Fiction)* Katie Gilbertson
"Stand-up," p.59 *(Fiction)* Sue Bruns
"Takeout on the Sly," p.37 *(Creative Nonfiction)*
   Victoria Lynn Smith

Humor (& Creative Nonfiction) Judge Elisa Korenne, a Yale Graduate and award-winning songwriter known for her original songs about oddballs in history, left New York City in 2006 to be an artist-in-residence in rural west central Minnesota. Since becoming a Minnesotan, Korenne has become known as a pioneering rural artist. She began her music career in 2001 after leaving her role at the international development nonprofit she co-founded, Geekcorps, an alternate Peacecorps for technology professionals building businesses in developing countries. Her debut book, *Hundred Miles to Nowhere: An Unlikely Love Story* was available June 2017.
www.elisakorenne.com

Reclaiming Life

Talking Stick 30

Poetry—First Place
Jana A. Bouma

Sunday Morning Samba

After John Calvin Rezmerski
What do you suppose
a lizard does on Sunday mornings?
Does he sleep in, read the paper,
ask for extra bacon with his espresso?
Does his swivel eye
light on the latest TV ad?
Does his long tongue flick across
the kitchen table
to fondly swipe a beloved snout?

Or does he rise to his full height, toes splayed,
belly white against the picture window,
scandalizing the neighbors?

Perhaps he busies himself
tightening the loose doorknob,
unclogging the stubborn drain,
peering toward the refrigerator's petulant squeal.

I hope that he grabs the missus
from behind, and that the two of them
go dancing dirty across the hallway's
cool, smooth tile, their tails twitching
the unpremeditated meter
of a swivel-hipped samba. I hope,
before the afternoon company shows up,
they slip away, strip off the old skins,
and slowly twine, the two of them,
swimming once again toward that old double helix
of Sunday morning desire.

Creative Nonfiction—First Place
Christina Joyce

At Rest

My father's snores were a force of nature, a tsunami of sound flooding the house each night. Sonorous waves washed over the darkened household, swirled through the upstairs hallway and down the staircase, before pooling in the living room below. Smaller tributaries of deep breathing flowed from the other three bedrooms. We were a family of seven, confluent in noisy slumber.

As teenagers, my siblings and I found Dad's soundtrack convenient when coming home past curfew. Getting in the front door was easy enough, but crossing the hardwood floors and climbing two flights of uncarpeted stairs undetected presented a challenge. Timing was everything. With shoes in hand, the latecomer would creak up the steps in rhythm with Dad's breathing. Inhale (step-step-step). Exhale (step-step). At the top of the stairs, victory often was snatched away when his disembodied voice intoned, "A little late, aren't you?"

Dad was always the first one up, even on weekends. With a fresh cup of coffee in one hand and the morning newspaper in the other, he'd enjoy the temporary peace before the rest of us lumbered downstairs. After a long day of teaching and coaching at the local high school, Dad would fall asleep after dinner correcting history quizzes or watching television. With his chin planted on his chest, his snores at these times were quieter. Even so, we sometimes raised the volume of the TV to hear our show. My mother, annoyed that he was dozing in the chair at 7:30 p.m., would wake him. "I wasn't sleeping," he'd grumble, picking up papers that had fallen to the floor.

For their anniversary one year, we gifted our folks an evening at the Guthrie to see *Rosencrantz and Guildenstern are Dead*, an existential comedy based on characters from *Hamlet*. Later, I asked how they enjoyed the show. Dad proclaimed it "interesting." Mom gave him a look and said, "Your father had a nice long nap." On this point, he conceded, deciding that it was nobler—and more harmonious—to accept the slings and arrows from his actions than oppose them.

The Halloween storm of 1991 hit Minnesota, like other parts of the country, and dumped a couple of feet of heavy snow that hampered trick-or-treaters and Twins fans still reveling in the team's World Series victory. It was also the day Dad, recently retired, was diagnosed with kidney failure and admitted to the hospital. From then on, dialysis became part of his routine three mornings a week. One of the side effects of his treatment was disrupted sleep. When he wasn't restlessly moving around at night he would sit for hours, sometimes reading, sometimes staring into the darkness. He'd drift off to sleep toward early morning and wake feeling anything but rested.

On the day he died, he slept quietly on the bed we set up in the sun room, his favorite room for reading and watching the world outside our house. He woke around noon, sitting on the edge of the bed with Mom, her arm around his shoulders and their heads pressed together. Nearly five years of dialysis and a couple of years of cancer treatment had taken their toll. But in that moment, Dad looked more rested than he had in years.

When he laid down a few minutes later, his snoring started in almost immediately. The sound ebbed and flowed throughout the afternoon and in the evening. We moved in and out of the circle of his breathing, attuned to its every nuance. Holding our breath, we waited for the next step.

Fiction—First Place
Anne M. Jackson

Charlie and Ruby

Seb frowned at the lonely bill in his violin case. The park was empty. Closing his case, he looped the strap over his shoulder. Today, he'd been playing whatever struck him, not the catchy tunes that moved hands to pockets. He turned from the park and headed towards the bus stop. He had dinner money or bus fare.

Passing closing shops, he decided to try the corner and see if he could turn his luck. He flipped off his wool cap and set it on a clean patch of pavement. He played his repertoire of slow dance. As the clerks went home, most dropped change as they passed. He tallied with his eyes. Dinner was served.

Squatting, he was storing the violin when someone said, "Are you done playing?"

He looked up at a small bent man.

"Yes, sir. Sorry for the bother. I'm moving on now," Seb said.

"Oh, no bother. We enjoyed it," he said. "My Ruby and I." He gestured up to a third-story window.

"That's great," Seb replied. Standing he said, "I've got to eat or my stomach will drown out my playing. Been a long day."

"You like lasagna?" the man asked.

"Yes, but . . . " Seb began.

"Some crusty bread and a touch of wine?" he added, with hopeful eyebrows.

"Sure, I guess . . . " Seb said.

"Great! Keep playing and I'll get dinner," he said and scurried back inside.

Seb perused the neighborhood. Lots of light. Nice enough cars. Retrieving his instrument, he played some old-fashioned songs, ones his mother had liked before she passed.

The man stepped out with a slab of lasagna, bread, and a glass of wine.

"Why don't you sit on the stoop here," he said. "I'm Charlie, by the way."

Seb stowed his violin and accepted the plate. He dug in. "Why feed me?"

"Ruby's ill. Hospice now. The window's open so she can feel the breeze and we heard you. She didn't wake, but she smiled."

"Cancer?"

"It's everywhere," Charlie said. "She's still my Ruby even if she barely wakes now. The nurses who come keep her medicated."

Seb nodded. "This is incredible. You cook?"

"Oh no, I do survival cooking only," Charlie said. "Folks from our church bring food, but how much can one eighty-year-old eat?" he asked. "It feels good to share it." They sat quietly for a few moments,

Seb stood to leave. Charlie asked, "You do this every day? Play?"

"Most."

"Would you come back?"

"Don't know. I'm never sure where the day will take me."

"If it brings you here, you'll have a full belly."

"I'll think about it."

"I'll see you tomorrow then."

"Maybe," Seb replied and left.

The next morning Seb listened to the news, drank coffee, and ate a stale bagel. Today had to be better if he was going to make rent. He was at his best morning spot by nine a.m., then moved to the park. He had to empty the cash from his case a few times to keep the ratio right. Too much money and people didn't give. Not enough and they thought he wasn't good.

By dusk, he could make rent and maybe restring his bow. He thought of Charlie and looked at the sky. The universe had been kind today. He walked to Charlie's corner and played. Charlie's beaming face popped out the window.

"Any requests?" Seb yelled up.

"'You Are My Sunshine,'" Charlie replied.

"You got it."

Seb played for a half-hour before Charlie appeared with two steaming plates of food. "Okay if I join you?" Charlie asked. Seb nodded and they settled on the stoop together.

"How long you been married?" Seb asked.

"Fifty-six years."

"Wow."

"You ever been married?"

"Nope. Never found the one. What's your secret?"

"No secret. Just find the one who knows you better than you know yourself and loves you anyway."

"That easy, huh?"

"Yup."

"How is she today?" Seb asked.

"Sleeping. I should probably go," Charlie said. "See you tomorrow?"

"I think so. Where else can I eat like this?"

Charlie grinned and stepped inside.

Seb wiped his hands and opened his case. Taking out his violin, he quietly played Brahms' "Cradle Song." Then Gershwin's "Summertime." He looked and saw Charlie in the window. Charlie put his hand over his heart and nodded. Seb nodded back and played softly and sweetly for an hour.

The next day he got to Charlie's early. He wasn't surprised by the ambulance at the curb. It pulled away as he approached and he asked a woman nearby what happened.

"Old man from 3C had a heart attack. They were working on him but he was long gone," she said.

"Charlie?" Seb asked.

"Yeah, I think that's it. You ask me, it was a broken heart. His wife passed last night."

The crowd dispersed and Seb was alone. He played "Amazing Grace" followed by "Swing Low." Evening settled around him and dusk painted the street. Seb looked up to Charlie's window and noticed a gray dove on the window sill. Another one landed and he stopped playing as they snuggled.

"They mate for life," a voice said near him.

Seb saw a man standing nearby. "Excuse me?"

"The doves. They're mourning doves. They mate for life."

"They sure do," Seb said.

Creative Nonfiction—First Place Humor
Tara Flaherty Guy

Rats

I'd been doing zoning administration in my rural Minnesota county for years and was fully acquainted with the love/hate relationship between citizens and local land use regulators, when I took a call one spring day from a disgruntled lake shore owner.

"I have a public health complaint . . . it concerns my idiot neighbor who constantly feeds those nasty ducks and geese down by the shore," she said. "He starts in April and doesn't stop until November. It's insane. *He's* insane," she further opined. "What do you plan to do?"

I was unruffled. In zoning world, citizen complaints always fell on one or the other side of the bright line; we were either doing way too much enforcement or far too little. We were power-grabbing commie dictators, or forest-raping, bunny-hating developers' puppets. The odd thing is, this was never a permanent philosophical stance; the same citizen could come down on either side, depending upon which of their oxen was getting gored on any particular day. This lady, though, was clearly deep in the *you're-not-doing-enough* camp.

"I'm sorry, ma'am, but we don't have a regulation prohibiting the feeding of waterfowl from private shoreland property. For many of our residents, it's part of the ambiance of living at the lake."

She was unpersuaded.

"Are you telling me that you people don't care that this nut keeps mountains of cracked corn in his garage for those damn ducks? It draws in vermin of all kinds to the neighborhood. I've caught giant RATS—not mice—RATS in my OWN garage, because of this freak's duck obsession. Plus, these effin' birds crap all over my beach. Would you want YOUR grandkids slopping through goose shit to get to their paddleboat?"

Admiring her undeniable way with words, I replied, "Of course not, ma'am, but as I said, we don't regulate the feeding of wildlife on private property. Maybe you could speak to your neighbor about keeping the cracked corn in airtight containers to avoid drawing in rodents?"

I could *hear* her bristling at my suggestion. "Oh, right. Fine. That's just *fine*. How *marvelous* to know that the county doesn't give a rat's ass about the health and well-being of its high-rent lakeshore taxpayers. How do I get a job like yours, where I can sit on my ass and do nothing to help the public? We'll just see about THAT, Missy." A click, then a dial tone.

Unperturbed, but assuming she'd be calling her county commissioner about my indifference to the depredations of the damned duck-feeders, I called and left word for the commissioner in question, tipping him a heads-up on his disgruntled constituent.

Two days later, a beautifully-coiffed woman wearing an Hermés scarf and a menacing smile better suited to a barracuda entered my office carrying a crackling paper bag, nearly sparking fury. As this was long ago, before government workers were protected by bulletproof glass at their front counters, she flounced over and *flumphed* down in the chair in front of my desk, in a choking cloud of Estée Lauder cologne.

"Good morning, ma'am. How can I help you today?" I asked pleasantly, despite my tingling danger antennae. I'd learned over the years to never show fear to an irate citizen, in keeping with the mad-dog defense. They would lunge for the soft throat.

"This is for you," she said, dropping the paper bag on my desk. Then she stood and whirled out in a throat-closing cloud of scent. In those pre-anthrax-greeting-card days, I picked up the bag and dumped out the contents. A half dozen frozen rats tumbled out and lay there on my desk blotter, staring at me with glittering, accusatory eyes. I stared back. Finally, after a long moment, admiring the dogged determination it had taken to make her point, I looked up, musing to myself and the empty air.

"I can't believe she put these in the freezer with her Tombstone pizzas and her Easter ham."

Poetry—Second Place
Mary Lou Brandvik

Losing the Wobble
Remember her first bike,
   shiny blue and grey
   with pink plastic
   handlebar
      streamers?

"Will you help me?" she asks.
And you do,
over and over
one sunny June day,
      running alongside,
      gasping for breath,
      holding her and the bike
      upright
as she wobbles side-to-side
down the driveway.
      "Don't let go," she cries.
      "I won't," you shout,
but suddenly the bike pulls away
and you are
      alone,
      bent over,
      gasping,
      hands on hips.

She never looks back but calls,
      "I'm doing it.
      "I can do it.
      "Watch me go!"

And you do.

Creative Nonfiction—Second Place
Darrell J. Pedersen

Five Young Men and Christmas 2020

A hairy arm, plaid flannel sleeve rolled up, extended out of the pickup window and held high a fist with middle finger raised. A week before Christmas, at the end of the tumultuous year 2020, I was headed for the dump. Driving where four lane transitions to two, loud rumbling engine acceleration caught my attention. *There he is, up ahead of me in the right lane, a big pickup.* Speeding up, he slid in front of a small car. That's when I spotted his obscene gesture. *What,* I wondered, *did that other driver do to earn that reaction?* Drawing close behind the little car, I spotted the offense. This little old lady had made the mistake of sporting a small presidential campaign sticker in her back window. I guessed giving her the finger was a victory for him.

Witnessing this attack on humanity by a bearded young man in a big pickup caused me to reflect on his place in our society and world. I thought about the large number of bearded young men I had lately witnessed in televised protests, a few packing assault rifles. Some recently shouted obscenities at me and others for standing in silent support of Black Lives Matter. I wondered, *has this whole generation been lost?* But then I recalled, *my own son is bearded and drives a noisy, old jeep . . . And he's currently using his vocational skills to put together a virtual Christmas Eve service for his church . . .*

That was Friday. Today, Monday, my wife and I pulled into a long line outside Burger King. I immediately took notice of the young man ahead of us in the row. He was driving an old pickup, paint peeling off and rusty jagged holes in its fenders. Seeing him watching us in his mirror, I wondered if he was another of these young ruffians.

Behind us, a brand new, red Jeep slipped into line. In my mirror, I saw another young man driving. I noted huge tires, winch, fancy mirrors, decals, all the options. *Lots of money for that one,* I thought. *I wonder what kind of a job he has? I never had money to buy something like that when I was his age. I don't have money to buy something like that even at age sixty-eight.*

A long wait; we were one car back now. The young driver in the rusty pickup carried on an extended conversation with the window person whose hand held the outstretched plastic tub awaiting payment. *Is he hassling that poor cashier?* Finally, he put his credit card in the tub, received his food and drove away. Our turn. The twenty-something man in the window, masked, said, "Your meal has already been paid for. The fellow ahead of you took care of your bill."

"What?"

He repeated. Bill paid. Young man in the pickup truck. $17.84.

"Well, can I pay for the people behind me?"

"Yes, if you want to."

"Yes, please, let me pay for their bill." *His bill.* I remembered; it was the young fellow in the expensive Jeep. I handed the cashier my credit card and he rang it up.

"How much was it?"

"Just over three bucks."

"Well, can I pay for the next car too?"

"Sure."

"How much is that one?"

"That one is $24.95."

"Okay, thanks. That will be just fine."

Bill paid. Food delivered. Credit card returned. Ready to coast away, I looked my young fellow in the eye and offered, "Merry Christmas."

"Merry Christmas and God bless you," he replied.

"And God bless you too," I said to one of my new young friends at Burger King.

Five young men just before Christmas in 2020. Pandemic, political strife, racism . . . So much trouble all around. Five young men and an old guy. Maybe there's still hope.

Fiction—Second Place
Kate Bitters

Hills of Iron

We sat atop a taconite hill, Grandpa and me. Him, with a flask of brandy tucked inside his Carhartt jacket. Me, clutching an open can of Sprite. We looked across the rusty landscape of decades-old mining tailings. They reminded me of giant burial mounds—a tribute to the dead and dying mining towns across Minnesota's Iron Range.

Grandpa had placed a worn cotton blanket beneath us, the same one he used to protect his truck cab from Clancy's muddy paws. Clancy was a hunting dog and spent most of his life outdoors. *Animals are not meant for carpeting and couches*, Grandpa said. *God gave them thick fur coats for a reason.* He had carried this belief from the farm to the little plot of land he and Grandma had purchased when they retired. Grandpa always seemed too big for that house on its minuscule lawn. He pressed against the confines of his quarter-acre like yeasted bread dough ballooning against its container.

"You cold, Joshua?" Grandpa asked.

I tugged my stocking cap lower. "No," I lied. "I'm fine."

"Good."

His eyes swept the landscape. The stringy stands of aspen had turned butter-yellow—garish against the red taconite hills. Wind gusted and sent their leaves shivering, the pale branches swaying. I wished for my Walkman. I wished I could quiet my churning thoughts.

Grandpa took a pull of brandy and returned the flask to his pocket. I kept quiet. I knew he didn't take to idle chatter, and I had nothing profound to offer. Setting my Sprite aside, I began picking at the taconite pellets at my feet—pellets that were mostly iron, bound with clay.

I pressed the pellets into the ground, forming a "J" for my name. Grandpa watched and said nothing. We were supposed to be bonding. *You need to get to know your Grandpa*, my dad had said. *He's been through a lot. Ask him about the Navy and the second World War. Ask him how to predict rain by reading the clouds. Ask him how to weld a muffler.*

I didn't ask. I didn't know how.

"You doing well in school?" Grandpa asked.

"Yes. Mostly A's."

"Good. Do you have a favorite class?"

"I like political science."

Grandpa sniffed, and I knew I had given the wrong answer. Somehow, I always gave the wrong answer.

"Can't say I care much for politics," he said. "All that word-twisting and manipulation. What is a man without his integrity?"

I began to reply, but fell silent. Grandpa's eyes had already wandered back to the hilltops.

A red and white Coleman cooler sat on the ground between us. He opened it and handed me a ham and provolone sandwich, wrapped in parchment paper. We ate, staring across the iron hills. Was I supposed to look for something? Was I supposed to find meaning encoded in the new-growth forest and red rock?

If so, it was lost on me. I took another bite of sandwich and chewed slowly, letting the flavors meld over my tongue. Down the hill, an agonized screech cut the silence. I jolted and peered down the slope. Something thrashed on the ground, sending a flurry of dead leaves into the air.

Grandpa set his sandwich back in the cooler and stood. I did the same.

The screech pierced the air once more—a primal sound, full of fury and pain.

"What is it?" I asked.

"Red-tailed hawk. Looks to be injured."

"Should we help?" My heart pounded in my ears; my stomach twisted into a hard knot.

Grandpa met my eyes and frowned. Entire paragraphs were etched into the lines of his face. "Let's take a look."

We abandoned the cotton blanket and cooler and strode down the hill. By the time we reached the hawk, its thrashing had calmed to a few weak flutters. We stood several yards off and watched its chest rise and fall in heavy, labored breaths. One wing dangled limply and a laceration across its chest leaked blood.

I stepped forward, but Grandpa held out an arm and caught me.

"We have to do something," I pleaded. "It's dying."

Grandpa's blue eyes clouded, like a storm passing over the sea. "It's too late," he said.

"But—"

"I said it's too late. Do you think this is my first encounter with a dying animal?"

I wilted. The hawk was a giant animal, all brown and white feathers with a burnt-orange tail. Its hooked beak opened and closed, and its golden eye—

I swallowed. Its eye was fixed on me.

Tears gathered and threatened to spill. I wiped them away with a sleeve.

"Joshua," Grandpa said softly. "At this point, there's only one mercy we can offer this bird. Do you know what that is?"

I nodded.

"I'll take care of it, okay? It's cruel to let him suffer."

Grandpa stepped forward, and I squeezed my eyes shut. When I opened them, the bird lay still, its golden eye fixed on the heavens.

When Grandpa returned to my side, he clapped a hand on my shoulder. "The hawk may have died, Joshua, but he will live on. His flesh will feed a red fox or a raccoon. His blood and bones will nourish the soil. He will endure."

I looked up at Grandpa. Light filtered through the aspens and fell on his face. I saw him clearly.

Fiction—Second Place Humor

Anne M. Jackson

Cat on Fire

The first time he tried to burn down my house was a cozy November afternoon. I was sweater-bundled on the sofa with a book and blanket. My cup of tea and a candle completed the mood. I was deep into the book when I smelled burning hair. My hands went to my head. Finding no damage, I looked around the room and saw Roger, jumping off the table looking as surprised as I was that he was a little bit on fire. I leaped up, exploding my nest of comfort. Sensing trouble, Roger leaped to his favorite window perch, promptly starting the curtains on fire.

I caught him by the haunches as he lurched for his next source of ignition and shoved him on the throw rug, rolling him up in it and patting him. Not thrilled with my assistance, he scratched his way out. I turned to the curtains which were burning impressively. With a tug, I threw open the sliding glass door, tipped down the curtains, rod and all, and chucked them out the door. I shut the door and surveyed the damage.

Roger sat grooming his singed fur and looking at me with a "this is all your fault" glare. Roger's not good at owning the consequences of his actions. Not once has he apologized. I verified that nothing else was ablaze, blew out my candle, and placed it in the kitchen sink just to be safe. Once he stopped sulking about the indignity of rug rolling, Roger let me inspect him for damage. Besides a few patches of missing belly fur, he was unscathed. Roger isn't a pyromaniac so much as he's a thrill-seeker. The occasional ribbon on a stick or felt mouse will suffice most days, but when he gets a twinkle in his eye, I know Armageddon is near.

The second fire was an intervention. I hadn't burned a candle since the curtain incident a year or two prior. My love life had spiced up and tonight I'd planned a fancy Valentine's dinner at my

16

house for my special someone. Roger had met this special someone and been a twit, so he was locked in my spare bedroom for the occasion. I gave him treats. I'm not a monster.

The table was set, and I had two taper candles lit for romance. I'd ordered in dinner, because I'm not a cooking kind of girl, and it was all staged appropriately in my dishware. I wore a sparkly dress and frilly underthings that immediately left their post and wandered up/down to places they didn't belong.

In this state, I greeted my honey and we began the Valentine ritual. The drinking of wine, the opening of presents (I gave him chocolate, he gave me a cookbook), and then we sat down to dinner. I had given up on keeping my underthings in check. I figured my dress would just hold them on. So far so good. Mr. Wonderful excused himself mid-meal to use the restroom. I reminded him it was the second door on the left and poured more wine.

He returned, and I started towards him, but my frilly unders had navigated south and hobbled me at the thighs. I was deciding if having my underwear fall off was awful or sexy when I heard the silverware rattle on the table.

"Oh, I accidentally let out your cat," he said.

Turning, I saw Roger sniff at my plate, then stand. I swear he squared his shoulders before rubbing against the candle. I hopped back in the direction of the table and thought things might be okay as the candle was tall and Roger was below the flame. Then the little maniac arched his back and lit his fur on fire. He jumped from the table and ran under the sofa. I let the frillies fall and ran for the sofa, nearly knocking over Mr. Wonderful. I saw him track from my kicked-off panties (I know. Hot, right?), back to me as I dove frantically, reaching under the sofa. It was hot under there. Roger had set it on fire.

I singed my fingers, then lucked out and found his scruff. I dragged him out and rolled him on the carpet. I turned to the shocked Mr. Wonderful, who was just standing there. "Fire extinguisher. Under the sink," I shouted and pointed frantically to the kitchen. He buffered for a minute, then ran and banged open the cupboard, and came back with the device. He read the directions for five seconds before I took it from his hands, pulled the pin, and let it rip. This required releasing Roger, who climbed to his favorite perch to watch the melee. Seeing no more flames, I sat on the floor, covered in the blowback of extinguisher chemicals. My fingers were slightly charred, my dress was no longer sparkly, and I was bathed in a relieved sweat.

I put my face to the floor to confirm the fire was out. Mr. Wonderful chose this moment to grab my butt. I stood up and looked at Roger. I swear he looked smug. I took a deep breath and told my date, "You can go." I pressed the cookbook into his arms and added, "You can take this with you. I'm keeping the chocolate."

Poetry
Rani Bhattacharyya

Stained Glass Soul
Laid back,
I stare across the distance
to my popcorn ceiling,
and the rainbows appear.
Sliver-thin strips, blazing in an arc
radiating from a pane of window,
dusted still and calcified
from winter's hollow scratchings.

The creamy popcorn is streaked
sharply with angled reds hazing to a green/blue to purple,
echoing each other and ricocheting
in a design that transcends space
bounded within these walls.

The setting sun also illuminates a glass menagerie
of green, yellow, liquid brown and garnet
cluttering the window sills.
It shines through crystallized yellow and blue wings of angels,
the leaping legs of a stag, and sets a silent fire
to etchings on a brandy bottle.
Yet, it's the olive green flicker of a bass tail,
and the flutter of tri-colored butterfly wings
that holds my breath in.

The emerald feathered leaves
of the scented geranium, leaning into the light
pulls my heart up in my chest
and my breath comes back to me
clear and crisp, scented Sicilian Orange.
It's on the second exhale that I smile
recognizing my own stained glass soul
in the warming light of the spring evening.

Poetry
Marsh Muirhead

Therapy
With some help from a therapist
I've caught my tail,
have faced the facts, the bitter end
of what I've done, where I've been,
with time enough to make amends
to those I squeezed
and swallowed whole—
time to shed another skin,
old stripes for new,
some grace at last she says,
and takes my check
knowing good advice is hard to find,
that truth itself is sometimes blind.

Creative Nonfiction
Ryan M. Neely

The Woobie Box

They say cats are as smart as dogs. I don't know about that.
In the corner of our living room sits a cardboard box.
Its sides sag.
The flaps are creased.
Edges frayed.
It looks to be growing fur.
But we dare not throw it out.
It is a safe space.
A space to go when someone feels down.
Mistreated.
Threatened.
That someone is my cat: Ferdinand.

Ferdinand was born in 2012. He is a retired breed stud. And he's a cat. In no way can he be classified as a Millennial, but he is very much a delicate and precious snowflake.

If you clip his toenails, he runs straight to the box.

Medicate his ears? He recovers in the box.

Pick him up while not wearing a shirt so that his flocculent ruffles brush against your naked flesh—*blegh!* Off to the box he goes.

If there's a thunderstorm or an argument or a crying baby, the box is where he seeks comfort in the same way a toddler reaches for a favorite stuffed animal or a blanket. It is because of this similarity that we named Ferdinand's safe space "The Woobie Box."

Once he settles into the Woobie Box he turns his giant-lantern eyes on you. Accusing. Certain that whatever brought him there must be your fault.

And don't you dare touch him.

He's safe.

He's on home base.

The thing about Ferdinand is, now that he's retired from all that *boom-chicka-wah-wah,* he's let himself go. His once-svelte form has swelled—his stomach distended.

When we first adopted Ferdinand, his whiskers shaped a lush handlebar mustache. But as a cat's shape changes—to compensate for a cantaloupe growing in his belly, for example—his whiskers change shape with him.

Ferdinand's whiskers have surpassed the handlebar to reach a glorious, out of control Dali, longer than a ZZ Top beard.

Most afternoons he spirals himself into a tight bean to nap on the back of the sofa. His back paws tucked under his chin. His head resting on his own thigh.

The first time it happened I was in the kitchen and all I noticed was his body twitching and his tail thumping angrily.

The second time I was closer but only caught him jerking awake from the corner of my eye. By the time my full attention was on him, his glare was passing between me and his still-thumping tail, trying to decide which of us had woken him.

The third time I was watching. Intent.

He had just closed his eyes. His breathing was heavy and sonorous.

Then it happened. His curled-around body, with his head on his thigh, brought those exaggerated whiskers close enough to graze the tender flesh of his backside. Stabbing him in the butthole like some kind of bottle-brush enema.

Ferdinand lashed out.

He grabbed his tail with one paw. Then he twisted his body, rolling toward his back, reaching to grip his tail with the other paw as if trying to put the thing into a stranglehold.

But his new shape put him off balance. His bowling ball stomach pulled at him awkwardly.

Instead of ravaging his tail as he had intended, Ferdinand just kept rolling. Inertia pulling him right over the back of the sofa.

There was a plunk and pitiful *mou* and then the scramble of tiny cat paws working over the carpet. Racing to the corner of the living room.

To comfort and to safety.

To the Woobie Box.

I'm not saying that dogs are smarter than cats, but while Ferdinand glared at me from the box, brushing his paws over his whiskers as if devising some conspiracy theory to prove I was responsible for all his naptime woes, it occurred to me that I have never seen a dog wipe shit from its face only to lick it from his paw.

Poetry
Frances Ann Crowley

Haiku
There was a tree here
I swear—it was a huge elm.
Woodpecker is stumped.

Poetry
Janice Larson Braun

Favors
On summer mornings
Before the raspberries came in,
My grandma made me
Rhubarb sauce for breakfast.
It was sweet and tart—
A perfect start to the day.
And because I slept with her
In her big bed,
I got to use her chamber pot
Kept under her bed
Until my mother told me
I was big enough
To walk to the outhouse
Like everyone else.
A few years later
Grandma came to stay with us
And slept with me in my bed.
And every morning
I would help her get dressed,
Unrolling her thigh-high nylons
And attaching them
To her garter belt.
One morning she patted my leg
And told me quietly,
"You were always my favorite."

Poetry
Laura L. Hansen

A Curiosity of Crows
I wonder what they are looking for
as they pace across the field
in grid formation
like a search party
looking for a lost child
or piece of evidence.
Every once in a while
they pluck at the grass,
reverse direction, each
keeping to their assigned
square, maintaining protocol
but jaunty at the same time,
chests puffed out, sleek
in their black uniforms,
crows, searching in unison
for that one bright shiny thing,
an earring, a coin, a bit of
broken glass, anything
they can hold in their beak
and let prism in the sun,
these scavengers, these
searchers, these light bearers.

Poetry
Ruth M. Schmidt-Baeumler

Remember
Does the leaning pine pine for me when I'm gone,
the creek miss my attentive listening,
the animals await the sound of the screen door being slammed?
Do they watch patiently until I return to enjoy
a glimpse of me in their forest?

Will the white-breasted sparrow remember my mimic,
robins recall we warmed their nest with a bonfire,
the swing miss the pressure of my buttocks,
my parents' gravestone long to be scrubbed by me?

Will the cabin's air anticipate my presence and
the creek fill willingly for my bath?

Creative Nonfiction
Jennifer Hernandez

An Immigrant by Any Other Name

My Great-grandma Marion came to the United States from Norway in 1898 when she was six years old. I'd always known this. It was simply a part of her, like her crown of fluffy, white hair, her missing index finger lost to a corn binder in childhood, the molasses cookies she set out when we rode our bikes over to visit her apartment, the china doll that sat on her bed, the one her daughter had given to her when they were both adults because Great-grandma had always wanted one, but her parents didn't have that kind of money.

I was in eighth grade when I learned that Great-grandma's name wasn't actually Marion. She had been born Maren, but when she stepped off the steamer at Ellis Island and stood before the immigration officer, he decided that Maren was "too foreign" and wrote down Marion in the registry instead.

I was in eighth grade when I decided that I would name my first daughter Maren.

I have three sons.

I was a mother myself when I learned that six-year-old Maren had crossed the Atlantic on a steamship with several of her siblings and her mother. Her father had gone on ahead to America to get established first. My great-great-grandmother spent six weeks on a ship with a passel of small children for whom she was solely responsible, on her way to a new country that she had never seen, and where they spoke a language that she didn't understand.

When my boys were small, I'm not sure that I could have spent six weeks solo with them in the comfort of my own home without losing my temper, my patience, or my ever-loving mind.

That was before the pandemic.

My own border crossings have been by choice, driven not by hardship at home, but rather by an impulse for adventure, the desire to explore new places, ideas, and ways of seeing the world.

I've lived in England, Japan, and Mexico. But I always knew that I could come back home. Always knew that I would come back home.

And I was single, a young woman in my twenties. Independent. Free.

Most definitely not responsible for the health and welfare of young children.

Most definitely not a girl who crossed an ocean and lost her name.

Poetry
Lucy Tyrrell

Gichigami Regalia
Lake Superior sparkles—
fish scales and water
droplets catch the sun—
like three hundred sixty-five
jingle cones dancing little
swells of blue cloth.

Poetry—Honorable Mention
Anne Seltz

Suncatchers
After she died
another needed her bed
  the bulletin board smothered with photos
  the mirror with old flowers and notes stuck in the frame
  the bedside drawer filled with used Kleenex and unopened mail
  the dresser holding food-stained sweaters
all boxed or thrown
It took three of us fifteen minutes to do that

The last to go
her beloved suncatchers
  scattered over the window
  pouring prisms of color onto her bed
  helping her smile and remember
Couldn't they stay?
Couldn't something of her stay
  so the room could remember she'd been there?

Poetry
Stephanie Sanderson

The Old Appaloosa
The old appaloosa nudges,
his soft muzzle probing,
asking why I have come
to visit him here
in his morning pasture.
A breeze fans his tail hairs.
The mottled shade dances,
making new patterns on his dappled
coat.
Ah, I say. I come to join you—
to feel life breathe softly on my skin,
to feel the color of sky in my bones.

Creative Nonfiction
Cindy Fox

Grandma's Wedding Ring

I wear two rings on my left hand; one is my grandmother's simple gold wedding band, the other a diamond wedding ring from my husband Jim. Before we were married, the first time Jim met my grandmother was in the hospital shortly after she had a stroke.

I was afraid to look at my grandmother's contorted face as she was paralyzed on her left side. I looked at Jim and mouthed, "What should I say?"

He whispered, "Just talk to her about anything."

I grabbed Jim's hand as we stood next to the bed. "Grandma, this is my boyfriend Jim. He grew up on a farm, too." I beamed with pride and continued, "And he's from a large family, just like us." Approval glistened in her eyes and I felt a slight squeeze as I held her right hand.

Jim's gentle eyes spoke more than his words. "Nice to meet you. I've heard many wonderful things about you."

Because it was difficult to carry on a one-person conversation, I slipped into the past, revisiting a fun time I'd shared with my grandmother.

"Grandma, do you remember when we had a Fourth of July picnic at the lake and while eating our watermelon, I asked why the seeds were moving? You looked closer and said, 'Ishka! Those aren't seeds. They're ants!'" I forced myself to smile. "But we ate the watermelon anyway." For one second, I thought I heard her giggle.

But inside I was screaming, *Please don't die, Grandma.* Grandma's inert body was pulling my insides apart, breaking my heart, tears clouding my vision.

Grandma's vision had diminished years ago with cataracts. Once removed, they would creep back again, making her secluded world in her tiny apartment even smaller. Eyes squinting, she couldn't recognize me, but I remember her saying, "I always know who you are when you start talking, Cindy. You sound just like your mother." Her words made me feel good to know a part of my deceased mother was still with me. My voice was my mother's DNA.

Not knowing what a stroke victim is going through, I wondered if my grandmother thought I was her daughter, not her granddaughter. I hope she thought we were both there, because later that day, Grandma passed away.

Grandma's wedding band was passed down to her eldest daughter, my Aunt Arlene. When Arlene died years later, the ring was gifted to Grandma's eldest granddaughter—me. I wear it proudly on the same finger as my wedding ring. And I will carry on the tradition, but it will skip a generation since I don't have a daughter.

When my time draws near, my only granddaughter Ellie Mae will receive the ring. She's only six years old now, but when she gets older, I will tell her the watermelon story. I imagine we will giggle and a faint glimmer of her great-great-grandmother will pass on to her when I slip the ring on her finger.

Poetry—Honorable Mention
Christopher Mueller

Prairie Sky
My grandmother never asked for much
across all the years of courtship and the war
and marriage and children
and the deaths of two sons.

She put breakfast, dinner, and supper
on the table each day,
prayed each night,
served her community like a saint.

When they moved to town,
retired from the farming life,
she painted the kitchen
a dusty blue
against the oak cabinets
and laminate countertops.

That color of a prairie sky,
of what heaven must look like
when it is yearned for with such certainty.

Poetry
Kit Rohrbach

Within the Globe
Curved walls overhead
where sky should be.
Everything is made of glass.
My sheets shatter
when I lie down.
I kneel in the shards
to pick at a crack
near the base;
my nails are torn,
my fingers bleeding.

I could rest
if it weren't for questions.
How will I pay this month's rent?
What did he mean
when he said that?
Where did I put my glasses?
They curl around themselves,
echo from the arc
in a voice that sounds like mine.

I wait for a world
where the earth shakes,
snow falls,
and I can sleep.

Poetry
Sandra Kacher

Unpaid Fines
When you were three you wrapped
my leg in a knee-squeezing hug
and told me fifty-seven times you loved me.
After ten *I love you, Moms*, I swatted aside
your buzzing ardor, returned
to a book soon due to avoid
a fine I didn't want to pay.

When you tried to scale my bed
I longed to wrap you close, but
afraid I would slow your timely
launch (in sixteen years), I
dispatched you to your toddler bed.
I still hear you sliding to your room
in your footie pajamas.

Did I push too hard for early independence
when I showed you how to fix your milk
and Cheerios, then slipped next door
for coffee?

Earnest at six, you helped me weed,
proudly waved the stems of
creeping bellflower you'd pulled up.
Both neophytes in the dirt, we didn't know—
every piece of taproot left behind would
flower anew—invasive as regret.

Poetry
Sharon Harris

Then and Now
then
I craved the dance
I craved the drink
losing myself in the thrill
of a new body pressed against mine
anticipating the rush of pleasure
the need to get closer and closer

evenings full of black holes
unsure how I got home some nights
waking up next to a stranger
our limbs tangled together
his face just a shadow

now
no concerts, no shows, no music
this world is alien to me
this world of no touching
this world where we stay apart
this world of no trust

no more random skin to skin
hands are gloved
faces hidden by masks
voices clouded and obscured
no smiles
and I stay in my home
afraid to go out

Creative Nonfiction—Honorable Mention Humor
Victoria Lynn Smith

Takeout on the Sly

Because of subzero temperatures, you warm up your van before loading up your two dogs so they can have a ride. Kindness to pets—you can put that in your *nice* column.

Your husband's at work and doesn't know you're going to the local bookstore today to pick up books you ordered. But he knows you bought them. You made a Valentine's agreement: He got a power tool and you got some books. Honesty instead of smokescreens about your book-buying habits—you can put that in your *trustworthiness* column.

You think about the restaurant next to the bookstore, craving a hot sandwich, something gooey, salty, and crispy. While the van is warming up, you find the restaurant's menu online, deciding on a grilled ham and cheese.

Your husband isn't home to know you're getting takeout.

He's at work, probably eating his cold sandwich as you pull up at the drive-through window to order your contraband. You're the one who declared February's discretionary budget maxed out. Unabashed, you order anyway—you ought to put that in your *naughty* column with a bold check mark.

You tell the cashier you're also picking up books from the bookstore.

"Park by the bookstore," she says. "We'll run your sandwich out to you when it's done."

You thank her. Pandemic-driven curbside pickups have advantages in subzero weather.

You text the bookstore, telling them you're in the parking lot. Everything's going nicely.

Then one dog barfs, and the other dog retreats to the back of the van.

"I knew it," you say. "I'm being punished for sneaking takeout."

But you're thinking, *Don't be ridiculous.*

You stopped going to church years ago but remember being taught as a child that the unrepentant are punished, and ten minutes ago you ordered an *ignore-the-budget-and-don't-tell-your-husband* takeout without remorse.

You clean up the barf with paper towels, then wait for your food and books.

The waiter shows up at your van *while* the bookstore is calling *while* the dog who barfed starts barking. You open your door, answer your phone, and tell your dog, *Hush!*

The waiter slips your order through the door and asks, "Is your window frozen?" The clerk on the phone asks, "Do you want a bag?" The dog barks louder.

You thank the waiter, ignoring his question about your window. You apologize to the clerk for the noise, saying, *Yes,* to the bag. The dog keeps barking.

You muse, *Without takeout there'd be no waiter. No barking dog.* You ponder. *More punishment for sneaking takeout?*

You've got your food and your books, and your dog has stopped barking. Maybe retribution is complete.

Ha.

Six blocks down the road the same dog barfs again, thankfully on an old towel covering the floor. You pull over and wrap the vomit up in the towel, which is going in the garbage when you get home. You're not cleaning up punishment puke sent from Above.

You glance at the sky, rationalizing. "It was just a sandwich—no fries, no soda, no dessert. I'm sorry I ordered it."

You wonder if God detects the annoyance in your voice.

At home, you turn the dogs loose, toss the balled-up towel in the garbage, and tote your books and takeout into the house. You shed your winter gear.

You bite into your sandwich. It's not ham and cheese.

You lift the top piece of bread. Slivers of beets litter the sandwich, soaking the bread with beet juice. You loathe beets.

Someone got your ham and cheese sandwich. You got someone's beet sandwich. There's meat on the sandwich but so many beets and no cheese.

You pick off the beets. Two pieces of bread stained reddish purple and scattered with pieces of pork remain. You think about throwing it out, but that's another sin.

You eat the sandwich. It's atonement for your clandestine takeout.

Confession won't be required.

Poetry
Liz Minette

A Space
The fog blanks out the harbor,
blanks out the lake—a space,
never a wall, but—
a space to write,
to re-write

anything

Poetry
Susan Coultrap-McQuin

Ode to Winter

Salmon light smudges
the rim of the sky,
spreads like smoke
in the faint blue dawn.

In search of food,
a gray squirrel scampers,
threading in the maze
from nest to ground.

A single skater dashes
over the frozen pond,
chases a black puck
around holes for fish,

then shoots to score
before gliding back
in loops of slow joy—
the color of dawn.

Poetry
Laura Krueger-Kochmann

Days of Art and Craft

my words splash bold color against the canvas
they splatter and shimmer and exist
life taking shape and form
its essence painted like a portrait

or like fingertips at the potter's wheel
words form wet clay into a vessel
creating a space to hold my ideas
capture the language of feeling

at times I labor to stitch the words together
woven fabric with texture of meaning
holding firmly to the warmth and softness
the utility and beauty

each poem a piece of the collection
shared at a price only
I know

Poetry
Mike Lein

Old-Timer
The bare black ground of the field, his canvas.
The leather-harnessed horses and the steel plow, his brushes.
The fine work of a straight furrow, his vanity.
The grain, rising to greet the summer sun, his masterpiece.

Poetry
Jeanne Emrich

The Rainbow Rises
The rainbow rises
as the sun lowers.
If I were early human,
I'd be drumming bones
just about now.

Fiction
Marc Burgett

Joyride

"Don't you move from that seat. You owe me ten thousand dollars. I'm gonna take a leak while you come up with a payment plan."

The mayor of Cold River, Minnesota, my high school drinking buddy, former employer and now my worst nightmare, sauntered into the stinking toilet of the Lonely Moose Bar & Grill, leaving me with a sack full of problems and no solutions.

Outside the window, framed by two neon signs hawking Hamm's Beer and Leinenkugel's, sat his pride and joy—a mint condition 1966 T-Bird convertible the color of a Fort Knox gold bar. It gleamed in the sunlight. The top was down, revealing black leather seats as soft and inviting as a woman's touch. The keys, I knew, were in the ignition. They always were.

"Who's gonna steal it?" he'd boast. "I own this town and the cops and their big, speedy patrol cars. How far you think a thief could get?"

I downed the rest of my beer, stood and walked to the door. *We'll see, you son of a bitch,* I muttered. *Put it on my tab.*

Poetry—Honorable Mention
Dawn Loeffler

Things Owned by the Man Who Made Me
Alberto VO5 with a black pocket comb
A pack of Camels rolled into the shoulder of a white T-shirt
A silver photo charm whose center spun from his baby to her
    mother
Auto grease-stained hands
Lava, Goop, and Gojo
Tony, in script, on his left deltoid

Emerald green '57 Chevy
Old Spice aftershave
A golden lion's head with ruby vision and diamond taste buds
Mock turtlenecks and a handlebar mustache
Weight bench and dumbbells

A worn thin black leather wallet
Holding $5 for the gas tank, a scratch-off ticket, and photos of
    his boys
Rolled-up shorts, blanched chicken legs, half-calf socks
Tinted glasses to hide his blind eye

A semi-truck
A gas station in the smallest town in the world
A door that opened to face a mountain
A motorcycle
A run-down trailer house
On ground that wouldn't grow grass

Faded, shaved-heeled cowboy boots
An oxygen tube
A pint of vodka—just in case
A morphine drip
A hole in the ground

Poetry
Marlys Guimaraes

Skating on Saturday
Music swept across the ice as my
skates slid on the smooth sheen.

I skated until my toes numbed,
the itchy wool socks not warm enough,

yet, I refused to stop twirling to the music.
When the cold became unbearable,

I joined the other skaters that
thunk, thunk, thunked across

the wooden floor of the warming house.
We sat on benches that lined the

walls and removed skates and
socks to rub feet that now hurt.

Pain was no deterrent, no reason
to go home. Darkness came, spotlights

reflected off the ice. I was hungry,
lusted after warming house cocoa and

large dill pickles in a jar on the counter.
Even with no money, it was enough

to glide on second-hand skates toed
with handmade purple and pink pompoms

that shimmered as I looped around
and around. And when that boy reached

out his leather-gloved hand, I grabbed it
and hung on—for thirty years.

Poetry
Mary Scully Whitaker

Oink Joint Road, 1/2 mile Ahead on Right
I s'pose it's a pig farm
which I should smell presently—
That pungent, sour smell
making the neighbors wish for a strong north wind,
minimizing the odor and carrying
it away on the breeze,
to sting the noses of neighbors to the south.

Or maybe it's a restaurant
that serves bacon and sausage
and ham and pork chops and
pulled pork with pork and beans
and barbecued pork and pork dumplings
and pork marsala and roast pork
and sweet and sour pork and pork pie.

Or maybe it's a saloon
where men get drunk, talk foul,
throw darts and pat the waitress
on her bottom while staring at her cleavage.
Or perhaps they are
playing pool and hustling
the young naive newcomer.

Or maybe it's just a road
like hundreds of other roads
crossing Highway 10. This one
on the outskirts of Wadena, Minnesota,
wanting to be remembered
long after the street sign has vanished
from my rear-view mirror.

46

Creative Nonfiction
Ramae Hamrin

Math and Science

I was a child of scientists. My parents met when my mom was working on her PhD in biology, and Dad was her organic chemistry professor. They moved to northern Minnesota in the late 1960s to start a life together. I was born shortly after.

Dad applied his expertise in math and science to build our house and raise much of our food—all in addition to his university teaching job. As far as he was concerned, science and math were the only two subjects that truly mattered. I knew before I was five that I would be getting a PhD in either.

Funny thing is, the twinkle in Dad's eye didn't come from grading papers or feeding cows—or even me. It was music. I caught glimpses of it as he listened to "Madame Butterfly" and Mozart on his reel to reel.

He loved to play music too. I watched adoringly as he strummed James Taylor songs on his guitar and hammered out Scott Joplin rags on our upright piano. And oh, how he loved singing in barbershop quartets. Some of my favorite childhood memories involve the two of us harmonizing to "Found a Peanut" on the long drives into town.

My parents' chemistry eventually wore off, and they divorced when I was ten. Dad moved away to teach at another university, and I only saw him a few times a year after that. But when I did, he would ask how I was doing—in math and science.

And I always did well in his two prized subjects. I even went to college—*his college*—for math. I didn't love it, but I seemed to have acquired his knack for it. As I washed laundry at his house on Sundays, we would cheer for the Vikings and talk about the two important things in life. I was struggling with anxiety and depression, but I was killing it in math and science.

Years later I earned my math degree, got married, and went to graduate school to finally get my PhD. But after suffering a late miscarriage, I left with a Master's, heartbroken, to start a family of my own.

Dad never understood why I would give up a career in math and science—to take care of children, no less. But he consoled himself with renewed hope in his grandkids, as he had once done with me.

When I divorced, I tried to explain to Dad why I had to at least *try* to get happy. I'm pretty sure he never understood. He also didn't understand why I wouldn't use such an opportunity to go back and finish that PhD.

I didn't see much of him after that. I went to work as a high school math teacher. It was math all right, but we both knew it wasn't the stuff his dreams were made of. He would show up occasionally for the kids' track meets and orchestra concerts, but he never made the drive just to see me.

Dad died of cancer before the girls graduated from high school and before learning they would go on to study his beloved classical music in college. And he died before science had a fighting chance to save him.

He died before getting to know the daughter who so desperately tried to please him. He died before learning that she would soon be diagnosed with cancer too.

I quit my teaching job and have little to do with math and science these days. Instead, I became a writer. And in those quiet moments when I sit down to write, when I contemplate living and dying, I hear him whisper something we both now understand. *It's math and science that will extend my life, but it's listening to the music in my soul that will save it.*

Poetry
Dawn Loeffler

New Perspectives
I watched Mom's fingers stroke
the mother of pearl reading glasses
a small upturn of her lips with each touch
reminding me of her times with Dad

The next day the glasses and Mom's heart
were shattered on the kitchen tile
She was inconsolable for months
vowing never to own another pair

Slowly need overpowered will
She returned with a shocking red pair
saying it flirted with her unique disposition
She was strikingly fond until Red took flight
from the hood of Mom's car
Scratched and dented they tried to persevere

Until lunch with a friend
an introduction to a multicolored beauty
Smooth-talking salads later
Multi was installed, Red in recycling

I caught Mom at her 55+ volunteer job the other day
I had to chuckle
She wore a classic black reader on her nose
a hot pink pair holding back her hair
and a polka dot pair hanging from the neckline of her T-shirt
She looked left and smiled—looked right and smiled
"What?" She shrugged
"I know, finally, that it is best to always have a back-up."
And she winked at me

Poetry
Amanda Valerie Judd

New to You
"Used books"
but not used up,
maybe just used
to being shelved and never touched.

Not "new and improved,"
nor "used and abused,"
just a little bruised
from being previously perused.

Perhaps misused
and now refused,
those books used to be
the stars of the library.

Fiction
Adrian Potter

The Difference Between Narrator and Author

I hand my mother a copy of my first book with a disclaimer. *Where it says I, that's not always me.*

Later Mom cross-examines me about my replicas, assembled from crude metaphors and poetic license. She gets hung up on each sonnet's mythology like a bed sheet on a clothesline. My clones walk past and ignore my mother, untethered to identity. I wish I could claim I mourned each one with their leather jackets and dubious attitudes, but they start to pile up in the poems like garbage. So heavy that I can't lug them more than a few feet without pausing. Until I finally douse them with gasoline and light them ablaze.

Where it says I, that's not always me.

I gently echo this explanation of a literary device, feeling guilty for secretly wishing I could become one of my poetic duplicates, no longer duty-bound to repeat myself to a mother who can hear but never fully understand me.

Poetry
Tim J. Brennan

Optography
Walking County 105,
you pass beneath a tree
you can't name—
faint smell of honey, a frayed
calling of magpies

and you remember
a walk earlier around Cavalry,
the day's rays of early summer
losing energy in a brief Minnesota
drizzle, cooling snap dragons
as curious as people are—

there's a feeling you've left
something behind so you stop
and walk back a few steps—

maybe the hum of a distant windmill,
it turns out to be a swelling,
a black-and-white hive,
exhaling drones—

some as burnished as museum doubloons
from a Spanish galleon, and behind the comb
a new summer tang, the sun's penumbra
dipping behind the hill and the far trees

leaving an after-image as you look ahead,
about as long as the moment that created it.

Poetry
Norita Dittberner-Jax

The Gift
Softness on a cold clear day, trees lift
their bony branches, clean snow
and ice.

I drop off a birthday gift
to our granddaughter, the two of us
sending out smiles behind our masks.

On the way home, I pass the VA,
the kindly faces of the staff, the labyrinth
we knew by heart.

A wrong turn, I'm circling
the airport where the doors slid open
for us, our best coupledom.

Your body and mine, our loving. I drive home
in that tenderness and it lasts all day and for once
you're not at the cemetery.

Poetry
Joanne Cress

Beyond
A ripple of black and white
moves across
an emerald green sea.

Mother skunk and four little ones
hurry toward a pebbled patio
to dine on food for feline friends.

Wind catches their hoisted sails
tossing them
in rudderless ways.

Satisfied, they recede
to their home in the depths
beyond the sea of emerald green.

Creative Nonfiction
Cindy Fox

Meeting the Neighbors

Retiring to the country, I cherished tranquility, yet feared isolation. Would the Dead-End sign on our road read Stop sign and no one would come calling? Or, would the sign lure in strangers of questionable character who searched for something to steal? When the UPS driver said his GPS stopped working when he approached the sign, I knew we lived at the end of the world.

Eventually word seeped through the countryside that my husband Jim could fix anything, a welcome sign for neighboring farmers. Jim, a mechanic by trade, was dubbed "Wrench" years ago. Today, he's still wrenching.

Our neighbor nicknamed "Hush" hauls in tractors and trucks for physical exams and, if warranted, surgery. One day over a cup of coffee, our conversation veered from mechanical to sentimental things. When he said he had the best wife in the whole world, how could you not like a guy like that? He and his wife Tina work together. Bale hay. Pick rocks. Butcher chickens. Help Black Angus cows give birth in the frigid air of early spring. A labor of love. At night she helps the children with their homework. No surprise they all make the honor roll.

Ron, also recently retired, plants a two-acre pickle patch each year, and cans hundreds of jars of itty-bitty dills which he generously shares with us. His wife Julie is a homebody like me. I wondered if we'd ever meet but, one day, while I dug in a clearance bin at the hardware store, Ron walked by and introduced me to his sweetie. We had so much in common, like losing our footing. I'd recently fallen flat on my back on our icy driveway while walking to the mailbox. Julie had tripped and tumbled down their basement steps with an armload of Christmas decorations. Before leaving, we simultaneously said *Take care*. And meant it.

Howie is the "rich" farmer, though you'd never know it with his down-to-earth demeanor. He and his wife Jan work in tandem on dual-wheel John Deere tractors baling hay, harvesting oats, and chopping silage in record time. Restless with nothing to do during the winter but feed their beef cattle, they recently vacationed in Reno, but couldn't wait to come home. Too much traffic, too many bright lights, too worried the cattle were missing them. But I had an inkling it was the other way around.

During the holidays, Jim and I reminisced about fruit cake and deep-fried doughnuts our mothers used to make. The next day Howie drove into our yard with these delectable treats. How did they know what our taste buds were craving? Then Hush and Tina dropped by with farm fresh eggs and several packages of steaks to thank Jim for fixing their machinery.

While Jim tinkers in his shop, I take advantage of quiet time and will myself to get some meaningful words on paper, a daunting task for a writer sometimes. I'm glad we live tucked away at our wilderness home which suits our hobbies.

The Dead-End road sign is now more like a marker. When giving directions to newcomers, we tell them when you see the Dead-End sign, keep driving until the road ends. Yes, our place tucked in the woods may be the end of the world, but thanks to our neighbors, we also live on top of the world—alone but never lonely.

Poetry
Richard Fenton Sederstrom

Leaflight
for Carol
We walk our road again
with purpose-seeming steadiness
until we reach the deeper ruts,
the road-side windbreaks and obstacles—
trodden crumbling emblems of the continents of time.

Hummocks and ruts serve to catch and hold
the first wind-blown leaf-fall: maple, birch, aspen.
We also catch at the falling leaves,
as many as we can hold away from their fate.

We hold the leaves in the outside hands,
the hands that aren't holding each other,
children's hands again.

Then, children for only another vapor of breath,
we toss leaves: maple, birch, aspen,
until we are covered like Egyptian birds
painted in titanium iridescence.

                    *

Without feet leaving the path
we rise in our sheen of leaves and fly
into the freedom—
rarer, shorter each year now—leaves
Claret and Rhenish, well-aged life
in the colors of wine.

You gesture a silent trick of question
and I ask where.
You beckon to show me.

Poetry
Linda Maki

Gone
My mother called
  every day
    to ask
      what
        I was fixing
          for dinner
that night.
        And she truly cared.
         I miss that more than anything.

Fiction—Honorable Mention Humor
Sue Bruns

Stand-up

Sarah had arrived at Prairie Home Living Apartments in time to hear, "Ladies and gentlemen: Bigs Golden!"

"Your dad's up," her mom said.

"No, they just introduced—Bigs somebody."

"That's your dad's stage name."

"Stage name?"

The two of them watched from the back of the room as "Bigs" ambled up the ramp onto the stage.

"A duck walks into a bar," he started.

"Geez, Mom, is he really going to tell that joke?"

"Shhhhhh." Elizabeth held her forefinger to her lips and half-frowned at her daughter.

"I can't believe Dad's doing this," Sarah said.

"He's always wanted to do stand up," Elizabeth said. "You know that."

"No, Mom, I don't know that. Dad's terrible at telling jokes. He either gets the details out of order or messes up the punchline. Aren't you afraid he'll embarrass himself up there?"

"He's been up there before. They love him."

"I just don't want him to be humiliated," Sarah said.

"He's got to pursue his passion. He's eighty-four. If not now, when?"

Bigs, a retired accountant, was a good father. He laughed often and found humor in little things, but he had no sense of timing and often stumbled over words.

"Then the bartender said, 'I'll put it . . . on your . . . tab.'"

"No, no. I knew he would screw it up. It's 'bill,' not '**tab**.' 'I'll put it on your **BILL**!' It's a **duck**! Oh, Mom."

Her mother wasn't listening. She laughed and clapped with the rest of the audience. Gladys, in the front row, had snorted when she laughed, which made George and Dolores laugh, and then Dolores snorted, and that made George laugh harder until a bit of flatulence escaped him, which made everyone laugh even harder.

"Dad thinks they're laughing at his joke. Mom, rescue him!"

Her father stood on the stage, leaning on his walker, smiling broadly.

"Did you hear the one about . . . Ole on a plane from Minnesota . . . to Arizona?"

Her father went from one random joke to another—all of which she'd heard countless times. She couldn't bear to see him make a fool of himself, but Bigs plodded on.

"They'd gone about half . . . an hour when the pilot . . . said, 'Attention, please. We've lost one of our . . . engines. We're okay, but we'll be an hour . . . late to Phoenix.'"

Gladys was already laughing. Sarah wrung her hands. Her dad had said that line as if he had to breathe every other word. Was he having a heart attack? Maybe he was dying up there—figuratively and literally.

"Another half . . . hour later, the pilot . . . came on the intercom . . . again and said, 'We've lost another . . . engine. We'll be . . . two hours . . . late to . . . Phoenix.'"

Gladys chortled; Dolores sniggered. George was perched on the edge of his chair, one hand over his mouth. The entire audience was transfixed by Bigs. Elizabeth smiled, clutching her hands over her heart in admiration.

"Geez, Mom. Will he live through this joke? Can he make it to the punchline? Does he have an inhaler? An oxygen tank?"

Elizabeth turned toward her daughter. "He's taking his time to make sure he gets the details right," she said. "I don't know what you're so worked up about. Just relax and enjoy it. He's having the time of his life up there."

Sarah clamped her mouth shut and focused on her father.

"Another . . . half hour later, the pilot's . . . voice came over the . . . intercom again. 'I'm sorry, folks, but . . . we've lost **another** . . .

engine. We'll be **three** hours . . . late to Phoenix.'"

Gladys shrieked. Dolores was in tears. George slapped his knee in anticipation. Sarah watched from the back of the room. Everyone waited for the punchline they knew was coming. Elizabeth's repressed laughter came out in a series of chuckles; her entire body shook.

"'Gee,' Ole said, 'I . . . hope we don't lose that . . . last engine . . .'"

George couldn't hold it in any longer. His laughter exploded, interrupting the punchline, and Bigs paused before finishing.

"'Or . . . or we'll be up here . . . all day.'"

The entire room erupted. Gladys bent over, holding her sides. Dolores stood and cheered, "Bigs! Bigs!" Those who could, rose to their feet, most of them clutching canes or walkers for the standing ovation. George shuffled up to the stage. "That was the best ever, Bigs." He laughed. "I don't know how you do it!"

Gladys waddled off to the restroom. This much laughter always tested her bladder. Elizabeth worked her way to the front of the room as Bigs eased his walker down the ramp. She kissed him square on the mouth and wrapped her arms around him. He gripped the walker tightly with his left hand and hugged her with his right arm.

"They loved you, Bigs!" she said. "You were great!"

Sarah had moved up from the rear. Bigs smiled at his daughter.

"I'm so glad you could be here," he said. "I was really on my game tonight!"

Sarah smiled and hugged her dad. "I've never heard you tell it better, Dad," she said, and she wasn't lying.

"Can you stay another day?" he said. "Tomorrow is karaoke night."

"But you don't sing, Dad, do you?"

"Oh, no," he said. "But you know your mother's always dreamed of being a singer, and if not now, when?"

Poetry
Mary Kay Rummel

Blackbird Music

Rain always takes her by surprise, a frisson of pleasure
while that spit and hiss and rain-jazz mixes it up with
the chip and scold of finches mad at the sky going to pieces,
solid earth flowing away underneath their wings.
Inside, fire snaps with dusty burning smell of childhood
when she stood above the register, heat belling her nightgown
scorching her socks while she plotted escape from her brothers.
Their bullying chased her to word-made refuges in books.

Face against window glass, counting drops battering grass,
watching blackbirds in the downpour, she longs to be
more than human, taking flight, take her chances with the flock,
shaking out rain-logged feathers in sheltering banks of jasmine.
Childhood farther now than dying, she can't say more than this—
Now and then blackbird music, older than language, moves my
    tongue.

Poetry
Ben Westlie

Nature Boys
As kids
we wandered into woods like hitchhikers
knowing nobody would come for us.
We slept on tree stumps.
Found rocks that could be split open to gems or orbs.
You were hypnotized by birds.
What sound belonged to what beak?
Our tone-deaf ears praying for the correct melody.
I was more interested in the forest light.
Aureate brush.
Jeweled petals of wildflowers.
Ghostly trails with speckles of the sun—
that made us question our safety.

You were my compass.
You were my protector.
I needed so much from you.
Nature never harmed us.
Was it because we were characters,
brothers,
even friends?
Tell me how to listen to birds again.
Tell me how to notice our light outside our forest.
It was the blood under our skin that made us sing
in the language of the lost.

Poetry
Audrey Kletscher Helbling

Pandemic Pony Tail

Gray hair sweeps below my shoulders,
ends flipping in an upward curl
that looks more teenage style
than grandmotherly, which I am.

Sometimes I gather my lengthy hair
into a pony tail, a pandemic pony tail.
It feels almost comfortably normal
even in the absence of normal.

If I try, I can convince myself
that I look all right in longer hair.
But the mirror reveals truth.
I appear tired. Weary. Exhausted.

In my reflection, I recognize the stress
of living in a COVID-19 world.
Months of separation from family and friends.
No hugs or kisses or the closeness I crave.

I miss life as I once lived it—
gathering rather than distancing,
smiling rather than masking,
hugging rather than stretching arms.

I yearn to hug my daughter,
to kiss my mom, to embrace life,
and to watch scissors snip inches
from my much-too-long gray hair.

Creative Nonfiction
Niomi Rohn Phillips

Caged

At the onset of the pandemic, husband and I were living in our winter home in the Hawaiian Islands. Quarantines were strictly enforced, a fairly simple matter on our small island with only one major, two-lane highway. Patrols were set up to issue citations for disobeying the nine p.m. curfew and for travel other than to the grocery store or pharmacy. You could go to the beach IF you were going to exercise—to walk, that is. You could not get into the water nor sunbathe on the shore.

In spite of all the restrictions, we were free to meander the many miles of community paths with the ocean to horizon on one side, the crenelated, green mountains just beyond the valley on the other. We couldn't congregate, but we could wave to our friends and neighbors and enjoy a conversation at six-foot distance.

The statewide mask mandate was enforced. Shopping without a mask, unthinkable. We frequented the local grocery store at the six a.m. hour reserved for elders. A masked clerk stood at the door to enforce the mask policy, to monitor the number of people entering, and to spray every grocery cart with disinfectant.

We enjoyed our usual five p.m. cocktail and discovered Netflix.

Spring and time to go home. Masked airport personnel escorted us through the ghostly airport to the National Guard posted at the Delta gate. They took our temperatures before we could board the plane. Only twenty-five passengers on a flight that normally seated three hundred. Flight attendants and all passengers wore masks throughout the eight-hour flight. From that cocoon, we embarked into the eerie silence of a normally crowded airport and felt the fear of being in a foreign country. The maskless were everywhere.

At home in Minnesota, we were cautioned to avoid exposure to COVID at all costs. Death was imminent for people our age who got "it." Our daughter stocked the refrigerator, the cupboards, and the freezer.

Here we were in our beautiful Northwoods, the loons singing, the birches leafing out, and in the enviable position of having a daughter down the road. But that child became the parent. Freedom as we had known it was over. She was adamant about our "staying clean," as she put it. She stopped by every day for a list of errands and to make sure we didn't sneak out.

I yearned to roam the aisles of the grocery store instead of giving Daughter my list, although unpacking groceries was akin to Christmas. Surprises in every brown bag. Diet Coke on the list. Mineral water in the bag. Diet tonic on the list for fewer calories in my afternoon gin. "Diet drinks are unhealthy," she said. The real stuff is in the bag.

And the eggs—eighteen Large Cage-Free Brown Eggs. When I was sixteen years old, I worked in a small-town bakery. Early summer mornings, I sat on a low stool taking one egg at a time from a square crate, which contained twelve dozen eggs from a local farmer. For hours I cracked eggs for the day's baking into a large white plastic pail, recoiling at the traces of chicken shit on shells, stomach flipping at the brown spots of blood or bigger somethings oozing from the snot of egg whites. The smell of chicken feathers and raw egg in that stifling oven-heated room eclipsed the aroma of doughnuts frying. *I have never bought anything but white, washed, candled, inspected eggs.*

I googled *cage-free* and *free-range* and *free-to-forage*. What does it mean? Those chickens were free to roam. I would have to drive by Daughter's cabin to escape.

Poetry
Sue Bruns

Downside Up
Everything changes
when the world tips.

We lie on our backs on the slope of a hill,
clutching the grass, fearful of falling
into the abyss of the sky below.

V's of Canada geese skid upward onto the rippled lake.
Inverted willows catch the wind and sweep the clouds below us.
Bald eagles chitter and glide, their golden eyes staring up at us.

We watch, amazed, wondering when gravity would release us
and we'd tumble silently into the above below.

But we lie on our backs, looking down at the sky
as the sun sinks behind down-turned trees.
Pinhole stars emerge. Big Dipper
and Cassiopeia fade into view.

We let go the grass and remain on the hill
like soft magnets on a board,
like butterflies pinned in display.
We feel nothing; we're weightless.
The world continues to turn.
We let go of what we had known before.

Soon it isn't strange to see a full moon fall from the horizon,
a shooting star dart below us,
aurora borealis coaxing us north,
and wild horses eating the sky.

Poetry
Kristin Laurel

Two Tankas

Little Kingdom on the Rock
Deep woods, early spring.
The old green moss slowly grows,
soaking up dewdrops
in the damp shade. Such rootless
want, on this side of the grave.

Charmed
A pod sheds its seed,
a shiny brown buckeye waits
to be hand-picked. Such luck:
Its smooth dented space fits fine,
gives my thumb a perfect hug.

Poetry
Donna Isaac

Looking for Affection
Two dogs chained to a post
sat in the rain
outside a florist shop.
They were a little wet,
patient, soft whimpering.

Soon a bearded man
gripping jonquils and blue
cornflowers emerged
and loosed the tethers.
Dog tails whipped raindrops.

The man drew on a hoodie,
led the dogs down the sidewalk
with one hand and held onto
the bouquet with the other.
He was balanced by love.

Poetry—Honorable Mention
Joel Van Valin

Angel Light
Sounds like the name of a town
somewhere way up on the border, doesn't it?
Town with one street and a playground
scrawled near the top of the map.

You look like someone who might come from there
with your summertime blue jeans and careless
T-shirt. Take me with you
if you ever decide to go home.

Poetry
Marsha Foss

In This Very Cemetery
sometimes in high school
my boyfriend and I made out
as the blood-red blooming moon
came up over the pine trees
and the headstones.

Now the moon rises
on my parents' graves
in this very cemetery
and I wonder

whatever happened to Bill
after the terrible war
took him away
and returned him.

I look for his marker
as the moon grows smaller
the pine trees taller
near the veterans' section
by the wall.

Two terrible wars
fought under the same half-cocked moon,
two generations side by side
buried
under the same bloody moon
in this very cemetery.

Poetry
Amanda Valerie Judd

Reach the Beach
a blue cotton candy sky
cinnamon-colored skin
decorated with pink frosting triangles
mixed with coconut, Coppertone® and conch shells
walking on saltwater
high on happiness,
drunk on sunshine
all day, *From Here to Eternity* . . .
as far as the eye can see . . .
to the crimson citrus horizon
where it flows over the edge like a waterfall
no worries, no cares as we listen
to the subtle sounds of a thousand waves swirling
in the smallest of shells
tossed recklessly upon the black sand

Creative Nonfiction
Anne Stewart

Footprints

In Tanzania, archaeologists discovered the footprints of humans hardened in lava ash 3.6 million years ago.

Snow fell overnight. Sunrise, and the soft, gypsum-white snow is, as yet, without tracks.

Across my front deck, the marten, on its daily check of the bird feeder on the railing, will impress double prints of its quick, eager leaps in the snow. The small red squirrel's scurry will be decipherable in paw marks left on its way to the feeder, taking care not to encounter the marten.

This afternoon I will walk to the mailbox a mile away and leave a trail of rubber-boot-soled footprints. On the way I might intersect a trail of large paw prints made by the pack of wolves that shares my territory.

Perhaps this evening the fox will stipple single-file footprints in a neat, defined line in our driveway. I will marvel at how dainty they are, hope to catch a glimpse of her on her usually crepuscular circuit. A fisher may leave his signature.

Tonight, tomorrow, or next week, new snow will fall. The prints of the squirrel, the marten, the fox, the wolves, the fisher, and myself will be covered. We will again layer our routes, crisscrossing trails, a journal of each on our way to seek, to secure, and to endure.

We will trace the movement of our lives anew in fresh snow, again and again and throughout the winter—if the marten does not eat the squirrel, the fox does not eat the marten, the wolf does not eat the fox, if the fisher escapes peril, if I keep going for my mail.

In the spring melt, layer by layer our tracks will be exposed —for a brief time our history revealed.

Poetry
Kathleen J. Pettit

Spring
Grays and browns cover landscapes.
The sky hovers while cold frosts fingertips.
Surely there must be spring somewhere
with its melody of melting snow,
the faintest brush of green dusting barren branches,
and genteel rain washing away grit and debris.
How I long for the time of shedding layers,
the awakening, illuminating of empty fields and
trilling of birds on leafing trees.

Fiction
Edis Flowerday

The Rules of the Game

Michael lifted the shade enough to peek out at the snowy morning. It was still dark. When his plane had landed the previous evening, the temperature was -10° Fahrenheit. His dad watched him exit the terminal, and snorted. Michael was barefoot in loafers. No hat. No coat.

"Learn anything useful at that fancy college?" his dad asked.

Michael didn't answer.

The plan for that first day was to hit an estate sale. His dad said that Michael needed to learn the value of things and the rules of the game. "Grab a mug and some coffee. We need to hustle if we want good numbers." The ear flaps on his dad's sheepskin cap were down. Michael hated sheepskin caps with the ear flaps down. It looked so common.

Michael sat in the car warming his hands around the coffee mug, looking out at the dark. When his dad took a sharp right, coffee sloshed all over him. *How long before my jeans freeze?* he wondered. *Will they crack and shatter when I stand?*

Near the sale, they stopped mid-street. Michael's dad tooted the horn, and a woman came over, playing a flashlight on their faces. She handed over two scraps of paper.

"Thanks a heap, sweetheart," his dad said, giving one of them to Michael. It said #18. "Hang on to it. That baby's worth money." Michael put the slip in his mitten, and hoped his legs wouldn't freeze along with his jeans.

He was dozing when street noise woke him. A crowd had formed around a pickup where a man poured coffee and collected dollar bills.

"That guy's just turning a fast buck," Michael's dad said. "Taking advantage of people out in the cold. We'll get something after we have our numbers."

"I thought we had our numbers."

"We have the numbers before the official numbers. When we get them, we can leave. We have to be back, though, before our numbers are called, or it's to the end of the line. That's the rule."

The sun was just rising when a man came along, walking a schnauzer. He saw the sign—Estate Sale, Numbers at nine a.m.—and went up to the door.

"Damn! Let's go!" Michael's dad said.

Everyone hustled out of the cars and up to the house. They clustered around the schnauzer man, elbowing him down the line. The temporary numbers woman handed him a slip of paper, and he left, looking confused. They all went back to their cars, and turned on the heaters.

At the appointed hour, they got their official numbers, and peeled off to the nearest coffee shop. Michael's dad smacked the ad for the sale down on the table, and said, "Looks like a good'un. The old lady lived there sixty years. No heirs. Not even a cousin. Everything's for sale."

Michael asked, "So what are you looking for?"

His dad went silent for a minute. "That's another thing, son. You can ask me that, but never ask anyone else. Don't ask. Don't tell. And, if someone badmouths what you're buying, hang onto it tight. He wants it for himself. You can always leave a bid if the price is high, but don't bid a round number. Bid something like $56.87. It's the odd bid that wins."

Nothing in the ad appealed to Michael. Not the vintage clothing. He wasn't that kind of guy. Not the furniture or dishes. He lived in a dorm, and ate in a dining hall. The L.P.s could be good, but he didn't own a turntable or speakers. And what did ephemera mean?

They got into the sale with the first group. His dad and half a dozen other regulars formed a V-formation, and bullied their way into the living room. Michael wandered upstairs, where a guy was checking out the books. *Don't ask. Don't tell*, he thought.

He found a box of old black and white photographs. Shots of people in vintage clothing, riding in vintage cars. Scenes of cathedrals and famous landmarks like the Eiffel Tower and the Roman Coliseum. Young soldiers on trains, sticking their heads out the windows and waving. In one picture a couple of American G.I.s linked arms with a woman. On the back it said she was Marlene Dietrich. *Whoever that was.*

The guy looking at the books came over. "Hey, kid! Looks like you've found some stuff from the dead and buried past." *Don't let him talk you out of it.* The man went on. "Wish I'd seen that first." *He wants it, Hang tight.* But the guy took his pile of books and left.

Michael paid $25 for the photographs, and waited out in the cold. The man with the books came out, and asked, "Would you sell those photographs? Say for $50? You'd double your money."

"Make it $75," Michael said.

As he pocketed the cash, his dad came out with a couple of battered picture frames. "You didn't buy anything?" he asked. "Oh, well. At least you're learning the rules of the game, and how the system works. That counts for something."

Poetry
Mary A. Conrad

Crossed Stars
long before my time
other whimsical eyes
far past bedtime
played dot-to-dot
on the night sky
as the fire of stars
twisted and turned
around that velvet dance floor
revealing in the chaos of lights
patterns reflecting beloved
ancient myths of romance
intrigue and loss

modern eyes like mine
parched by digital light and
hungry for mythic connection
still search the celestial tapestry
for points of light that might form
the rose Juliet promised
"by any other name
would smell as sweet"
or fond Romeo's heart
"cut out in little stars"
as Juliet once called upon
the gentle night to do

Creative Nonfiction
Sharon Harris

Bonfire

My eyes rose from the glitter of the fire and traced a twisted journey across the faces around me. Friends and family circled the fire. The night surrounded us all.

My parched heart echoed with loneliness while all around me the voices rose and fell. Loud music swelled against my eardrums and pounded and pulsed in me while figures danced around the flames, throwing shadows. People laughed and shouted.

My eyes rose higher to the darkness above, to the chaos of the stars littering the sky. In this vast world, in this endless universe, where are you? And why aren't you here next to me?

Poetry—Honorable Mention
Tim J. Brennan

. . . to the World

Joy is an ephemeral,
briefly lasting
on the tongue-tip,
to the once or twice dip
of chocolate chip—

or to an a cappella singer
trying to explain pitch
to a pedestrian singer,
it may only last for a verse—

or maybe to the brain
circulating statistics
where none exists, yet persists
to calculate—

when all you want to be
is the rain that curls her hair
when walking with the woman
you love.

Creative Nonfiction
Christine Marcotte

Moonlight Reflections

From our home on the lake, I can see the moon and its reflection over the water. As the grieving months continue, I find comfort in the moonlight, no matter how fleeting, as it is where I sense my mother's presence. This feeling of connectedness is reassuring, like the notes she'd tucked into my school lunchbox when she knew I fretted about an upcoming test.

I haven't always felt this way about the moon. I was ten years old when Armstrong and Aldrin made their lunar landing on that Sunday in July. Dad required me to sit in front of the television to watch the historic moment. My brother, who had counted down the days for weeks, was denied the opportunity—Dad's petty meanness for a minor infraction. I wished I could have traded places with him.

My opinion of the moon has changed since then. I admire it, not because of what might be on it, but because of the tranquility I feel in its light. During the summer, I love to sit against a towering red pine and watch the moon move with precision across the lake until it is in front of me. Then, if the wind is just a whisper, I can see a path so beckoning that I am tempted to follow it across the water. The first time I saw this mesmerizing reflection, I went down the rocky embankment to the widest part of the moonbeam where the silvery light touched the shore. There, I felt centered and completely at peace.

Mom's interest in the moon also swayed me. She looked at it as an astrologer. She'd remind me during a full moon to be wary of emotional upheaval and thus to take an extra moment before responding to unpleasant situations. She also said that the best time to start a new project was during a new moon. I'd forgotten, until we were sorting her papers, that she had written *The Worried Moon*, an unpublished children's book about protecting and preserving the earth nearly thirty years ago. Mom worried too about many things, especially in her later years. And when something was on her mind, she needed to talk about it *now.* I was the first of her children to retire and she called me nearly every day. Sometimes the conversations were short. But, more often than not, they were lengthy, as I helped her sort out the what-ifs and maybes of her daily life. It was exhausting. However, upon reflection, I know how important it was to her well-being. One call I always appreciated was a reminder that, "Tomorrow is a full moon."

The *Onaaani Giizis*, the snow crust moon of the Ojibwe, is the March full moon. I pull back the sheer curtains of the floor-to-ceiling windows in the living room and nestle in a cocoon of blankets. I'll have my journal and a cup of hot tea within reach and my dog at my feet. I'll crack open the window, breathe in the crisp air, and begin a muted conversation.

In these midnight hours, I share with Mom how I am doing, ask advice, and try to determine where she is in the spiritual realm. Sometimes I receive no advice or a hint of her surroundings, but I reflect on how I am and what I might need. I find comfort in the ritual.

The grieving months linger, and I don't expect them to dissipate soon, but as long as I can see the full moon, I can feel at peace, reflect on Mom's wisdom, and bask in her ethereal presence.

Poetry—Editor's Choice
Jim Bohen

Taps
the bugle
mourns
another dusk.
another desolation
pays the interest

on its loan.
a burden of
misfortune,
a hush of
what's to come,

fill the horn
with a slow dark
bird heading for

a still dark grove.
knowing less
and less of youth,
more and more
of other truths,
dusk is just

another path
that isn't leading
home.

Poetry
Mary Fran Heitzman

Faithful Companion
Bent and gray
he leans
on his walker
eyes squinting
through macular degeneration.

Jointed metal click-clicks
across the room
where his companion waits
near the window,
basking in sunshine.

Shuffle, click,
shuffle, click
he crosses the room
in slow motion
almost rewind.

Like a faithful dog
his companion waits
unmoving, steady
until the bird-like weight
of the old man's hand
presses on the wooden arm.

And his rocker eases forward
obediently
to catch the wisdom
of the aged.

Poetry
Marlene Mattila Stoehr

Blood Lab Waiting Room, Mayo Clinic, Rochester
Most patients assemble by twos in this cavernous room;
others sit alone, spaced apart like teeth of a jack-o-lantern.
Like them, I stare ahead. I wait. I watch. I worry.
I see the man a few rows ahead gently pat a shoulder
and smile at the woman in the wheelchair next to him.
On oxygen, she manages only a faint acknowledgment.
A man slouches feebly in a rolling chair, his crocheted cap,
a whimsical camouflage pattern, dangles from the handles,
swaying slowly back and forth from his any movement.
A pair of red suspenders drapes loosely over his shoulders.
Marked in one-inch increments to mimic measuring tapes,
they cause me to wonder if any medical test, any medical tool,
will be able to measure the length of his remaining days.
His companion nibbles on a crumbly muffin and sips from
a copper-trimmed thermos. A tortoise-shell clip seeks to hold
her thinning gray hair in a bun atop her head.
At irregular intervals an attendant emerges from the back,
reaches for the amplifying phone on the wall, and requests
a named patient to go to Door 1, or to Door 2, or to Door 3.
To some, this test will mean an end to hope, to others, a miracle.
For at this facility miracles can happen. Here miracles do happen.

And each day, the scene repeats. This gathering of the despairing,
this assemblage of the hopeful.

Poetry
Sharon Chmielarz

At the Peoples' Bakery
The counter's bread basket sits marvelously empty.
The People are buying designer breads!
One asks, Any more with flax seed?

The baker prances before the oven. The People
are buying designer breads! One open mouth,
one customer asking, Any more multi grain?

The counter's bread basket sits empty,
as if on vacation. *Brinnnng* goes a bell,
and the oven door opens to a rack of breads.

Out they come, to be slipped into a paper sack
for the People. Ouch. The baker violently
flicks her fingers. Very hot designers.

The baker is paid to be burned and be patient
about it. The sack she hands me steams.
She won't slice the bread for me. Too hot.

When hot, bread sags and sticks if cut. Who
wants to eat a tortured slice? The People
want bread that stands up to the knife.

An oven-y fragrance floats from my sack,
warm bread! The baker's basket is full again.
That. is. my. breadbasket the baker sings

and rubs her belly. She whirls to the next
bread eater. *Sprouted or gluten free?* She sees
only love for loaves in the People's eyes.

Creative Nonfiction
Paula L Hari

The Way She Tells it

Mom liked to tell me the story of the day I almost died. She'd start with, "Have you ever heard the phrase, 'From your lips to God's ear?'" Then she'd flick open Dad's Zippo, hold it to the end of the Winston pinched between her full lips and inhale so hard the tip of the cigarette would glow red and pulse, just barely, like her mangled heart.

I knew the story. It happened to me. But her version, well, it is different than how I remember. These are the facts. It was cold, overcast, late autumn 1972. I wore a plaid romper with a white-collared shirt and my red shoes. I'd recently started kindergarten, and mother had just returned home after a lengthy stay at Mercy Hospital's psychiatric unit.

"I knew when I woke up that morning that you were gonna die." She looked at me hard, almost angry. "I knew it deep inside my aching soul." As I remember it, I wasn't home when she finally got out of bed that day, having been shuttled to the neighbors that morning, like every other morning during the many weeks of her convalescence when my father left for work. It was our new normal.

"I was so scared, so alone," she said and took a long drag on her cigarette. "So I called Monsignor." Monsignor Albert Davidsaver, our priest, who'd been in close correspondence with my family during the Year of the Unimaginable: the year my only siblings, Teresa Ann (1/10/70-7/19/71) and Dennis Joseph (4/27/72-8/18/72) died within nearly a year of one another.

"I called and sobbed that something awful was gonna happen to you and that he needed to come." I was, of course, safe and secure in Miss Waggoner's class, driven there by the neighbors and probably listening to story time. "He said if it was of comfort to me, then he would gladly come." She took a short puff and blew it out hard and mean. "I told him that if he didn't come, you would die."

The priest knew her state of mind, the darkness, the grief, the despair. She only believed in him, not God anymore. She flicked the long stem of ashes into the tray. "When he got here, we went and waited on the front porch. I smoked. He prayed." She inhaled, then picked a remnant of tobacco from her lip and added that our house, 521 Iowa Avenue, was perched nearly at the top of a steep hill and that a fall drizzle had soaked the pavement that afternoon.

"'Bout 3:30, I seen the neighbor's car pull up and park across the street. You got out the back door, and then it all happened so fast and slow at the same time. You—" She jabbed at me with the embers of her cigarette—"darted out between the cars. Garrison's car came barreling up the hill." Her hands shook so badly, the ashes fell and powdered the table between us. "I yelled 'Paula!' You froze right in the car's path." She inhaled so deep and so long that I felt she might never breathe again. "And then . . . " She exhaled. "Monsignor raised his right hand up, put his left to his heart and whispered, 'God, save this child.'" Her ragged breath swirled ashes across the table. "And just like that his prayer was answered. Isn't that something?" she said. "He asked and just like that the car stopped. Inches from you. On a hill. Even the drizzle stopped."

"What happened then, Mom?" I asked. This is the only part I remember completely.

She stubbed out the barely smoked Winston and said, with a look that could only be described as awe, "You didn't die. You walked across the sidewalk, up the stairs of the porch and asked Monsignor why I was crying again."

Poetry
Jim Bohen

The Wolf
Shovels recoil
from hard dry earth,
must drive hard
for every inch.

Pin pricks puff out
sunken chests.

The wolf,
lean as a lack
of nourishing rain,

is scratching at
the door again—

as hungry as
it's ever been.

Poetry
Amy C. Rea

Polar Vortex

No meteorologist am I
and so when I read
polar vortex and
low-pressure system I
think of energy vortexes and I
think of the peace
of the bitter cold keeping
me home, of the lulling
song of the wind, of the quiet
hours I'll spend
in turtleneck and sweatshirt,
two pairs of socks,
crocheted afghan from the seventies
tucked under my arms
as I read, read, read,
pausing only occasionally
to sip my coffee.

Poetry
Pamela Wolters

Post-Surgery Communion
In the pale light of an open refrigerator door,
the pets and I gather in midnight communion,
receive a spoonful of cat food,
accept an offering of leftover hot dish.
I sip the wine of sustaining water,
wash down the wafer of pain killer,
thankful for the communion of these saints,
mindful of the holy moment.

Poetry
Pam Whitfield

That Annoying Couple
We've become that annoying couple
that nobody wants to see out
in public: you know the type

holding hands everywhere
brushing up against each other
in elevators
sharing the same step, the same step!
on escalators

they smell vaguely of sex
or maybe you're imagining it
either way, it's unsettling

how he looks into her eyes
as they walk, and she blushes
how she tucks her hair
behind both ears
the gray tufts springing forward

him springing forward to kiss it
or to tuck his hand into her bottom
on the subway when no one—
no one but you—
is looking

get a room! you want to yell
but how can you say that
to your elders

so you grit your teeth
and shake your head
and wish your own bed
were not empty.

Creative Nonfiction
Kim M. Bowen

Wily as a Tick Trainer

"I'm sorry." I apologized tersely, bursting with suppressed justification about why I wasn't.

Customer service felt like a 100 lb. anchor weight as I checked 113 guests into our nineteen-cabin resort.

Our third season was 2003. An irate grandma had just finished berating me for not checking resort phone messages that day. Her adult daughter and husband had not yet arrived.

I was too exhausted to begin painting her a picture of a typical Saturday in the life of a Minnesota Mom & Pop resort owner: cleaning cabins all day, then greeting waves of weekly guests until ten p.m. There were kids to hug, stories to share, registrations to process. It was just me, checking them all in.

When Grandma came in late one Saturday, I wish I could have stopped, taken a breath, and really listened to what was behind her upset. Not to her words, or tone. "You don't know who's called all day? Don't you check?" I translated this to: "What kind of poorly operated resort are you conducting?" I am certain the flared nostrils and tightened lips effectively projected pique of being asked to play secretary. As I walked over to the landline, she steamed on her side of the counter. I steamed on mine. There was, indeed, a message from her daughter. I curtly relayed the news. She abruptly strode away.

I wish that instead of hearing accusation, I could have interpreted: "I'm scared my daughter's family may be in trouble." If I had been fully present in the moment, I likely would have processed that this woman perhaps had cause for concern. I had met her son-in-law.

I had been introduced to said son-in-law two years prior. Within a few minutes of acquaintance, Mr. V. slurped a soda pop I had just sold him, while simultaneously relaying a detailed story of his abduction by aliens. Spittles of medicinal-sweet root beer were easy to avoid; images of probes and needles were not. Two ladies from another cabin had inadvertently been eavesdropping while they shopped. I noticed an anxious exchange of whispers, then a tip-toeing skulk towards the exit. Before gently snicking the door closed, one turned with a considering expression, and mouthed, "We'll be back!"

During our second year, my husband was giving a weekly talk to an audience of nine guests on the lodge deck, a typically peaceful area overlooking the lake. Mr. V. suddenly bounded into the circle, brandishing a roll of toilet tissue. He screeched there were "ticks-in-the-toilet-paper and how-could-we-have-snuck-them-in? Bathroom-time-is-sacred-and-it-was-NOT-funny and what-were-we-gonna-do-about-it?" My husband asked if the family had picked wildflowers in the road ditches? Mr. V. responded vehemently, "No, no, no-ticks-crawling-on-us-only-inside-the-T.P.-see-see-see!"

None of the wide-eyed witnesses spied parasites dripping out of the violently waving roll in question. No little black drops of arachnid creepiness were flung about, willy-nilly. It was suggested Mr. V. toss the T.P. in the dumpster and request a new one when the lodge opened. According to the others with whom I chatted later, as soon as Mr. V. stomped off, my husband became inundated with snickering compliments about how wily we were to train ticks. Did we keep ticks as pets? Teach 'em hand signals? Maybe we posted signs in "tick-speak," alerting all eight-legged blood suckers in the vicinity, "PLEASE HEAD TO A PARTY IN THE POOPER—CABIN 12—*STAT!*"

It's almost twenty years later, and I don't know why a particular apology to a particular grandma stuck in my craw so deeply. I still feel ashamed I handled it so ungracefully.

I should have applied the advice of a spectator to the revelatory occurrence of our tick-training techniques. Life can be absurd, she considered. Lighten up and play. It sounded too oversimplified, I skeptically argued. I admitted uncertainty in how to handle contact with Mr. V.'s family upon check-out. It was instantly suggested we ponder porcupine pranks next.

Poetry
Jeanne Everhart

Driving on a Country Road
August in Minnesota, I think of
Moses parting the Red Sea.
On either side of this narrow gravel lane
a green wall of towering corn stalks
rolls over hills like waves swelling
in an infinite cornfield ocean.

Poetry
Erin Marsh

Stolen Poetry

I broke into the Bemidji Public Library on a clear night, hoping my theft would make the next evening's news. I grabbed three collections by local poets and every issue of *The New Yorker* I could fit neatly into my backpack. It would not do to overstuff the bag and risk a page from an article on modern poetry getting caught in the green zipper, ripping, landing on the cobbled sidewalk leading to my apartment building. I knew the author of the prose poems about area lakes would arrive before noon to ensure her book was displayed in a prime spot. It would not be there, prompting the poet to believe her words had been checked out for the first time in two years. The poet would ask Connie at the reference desk who checked out the book. The computer would indicate the book is still available. After scanning nearby shelves for her title, it would officially be declared missing. The poet would search out *The New Yorker* issue where one of her recent poems had been published, hoping it would soothe her. The stolen issues would cause alarm. The police would be called and inquire if anyone strange had been seen hanging around the magazine section, taking a special interest in *The New Yorker*—specifically the poems. Each librarian would have their suspect. A news broadcast out of Minneapolis would announce a substantial reward offered for the return of poetry.

96

Fiction—Honorable Mention Humor
Katie Gilbertson

Stupid Ramblings

As I have been submitting short stories for publication, I am perplexed by the number of pieces that are called all kinds of wonderful. No plot, no character development. No dialog. Just stupid ramblings. I decided I was going to write a short story called "Stupid Ramblings." I would incorporate every idiotic feature I despise and submit it.

Thirty minutes later I had a flash fiction piece of less than five hundred words. It was so ridiculous and so bad I submitted it under a fake name but used my real email address.

The man lives his life at the library. There, amid the books, some dusty and some not, he feeds his soul on the hushed librarian tones that remind him of high school. Back then the wooden desks beckoned him to higher learning as he anticipated a wonderful future that never happened. He thinks if he keeps going to the library he will find some kind of hope.

Today there is a young mother with a toddler picking out books the kid won't pay any attention to but the mother will feel like she is being a "good mom." There are teenagers at the computers. They got out of the house by telling their parents they needed the internet for homework, but they are really on Instagram and TikTok.

Flyers are posted everywhere advertising classes and events no one goes to.

People are reading in the upholstered chairs or holding mysterious meetings in the tiny conference rooms. He wonders if he would feel more alive if he booked himself a conference room.

Outside the library windows, people are scurrying around like they have somewhere to go, something to do, someone to get home to. He has none of that.

He gets up and goes to the restroom. He doesn't really need to go, but it makes him feel like he has a purpose. If he sits in his chair too long, he might become part of it, like a sculpture "Man In Chair." People will look at him, and they will give him the serious consideration he never had in life. They will try to find out who he is, why he looks so pensive. In fact, it would be a lot more attention than he gets now.

Back in the library, he sits and holds really still. He stares, doesn't move a muscle. The librarian announces softly over the loudspeaker that the library is closing. He doesn't move. When they turn off the lights, he is unnoticed. He sits there. The next morning he is still there. And so on the next day and the next. Eventually his skin begins to look rough, then develops a pattern. He stops thinking. His body hardens, turns the same color as the chair.

One day a library worker notices him and walks around him, musing, thinking of the deep philosophical ramifications of this figure. She makes a sign that says "Man In Chair." Somehow his last coherent thought is, "I wish I had a sandwich."

On March 19, I received the following email:

Thank you for your wonderful submission, "Stupid Ramblings." We are very impressed by the deep, sympathetic portrayal of the Man in the Chair. It is rare that a new, emerging author can capture such pathos in less than five hundred words. We will be publishing this fine piece in the August edition. Please furnish your address so we can send your payment of $100.00.

I needed to act fast. I created a new email for my fake name. I got a P.O. Box in a neighboring town. I ran to the bank and opened a pka (Professionally Known As) account. Within a week, I had the check in hand and deposited it in the bank, half-ashamed and half-amused.

This was too easy. I took aim at my other pet peeve—poetry. After searching for online poetry journals, I found one containing the nonsensical blather of people who like lots of words and it paid $25 per poem. Ten minutes later I had a poem:

Clouds are reflected in a big glass building.
They appear, they emerge, billowing but they are trapped,
> *entombed.*
Fish are ensnared in the lake.
The child thinks all the world is trapped.
Then a turtle crawled over his foot.

Twenty-five dollars later, I was on a poetry contest roll. I remember the common remark about modern art—"My six-year-old could do better." I didn't have a six-year-old, but I did have a seven-year-old goddaughter.

"Molly," I said. "Give me three words. Any words."

"Mommy, street, princess!"

She shines untouchable
A humble goddess of the asphalt jungle
Set apart by beauty yet doomed to repeat the life of her
> *mother*

I won first place and $1,000.

That publication wanted a photo of the contest winners. There was no way on God's green earth I would have my real face associated with my *nom de plume*, so I sent them a picture of my feet—one in a high heel and the other in a Sorel boot. They published it. It got many comments about the dual role of women and femininity vs. strength and so on. I can't remember ever laughing so hard. The truth is my left foot is fine, but my right foot has arthritic swelling which is why I covered it with the boot.

Poetry
Bernadette Hondl Thomasy

Pandemic Ears
Not the noblest of facial features,
ears stood out during the pandemic.
They kept our masks snug in place;
they kept uncut hair out of our faces.

News of suffering, death, despair
entered our ears, traveling
straight to hearts and minds.
Neighbors banged pots and pans
in New York City, sending encouragement
to ears of weary doctors and nurses.

These medical heroes replied:
Wear a mask, stay home, social distance.
But ears can only do so much
when people do not listen; more grandparents,
fathers, mothers, brothers, sisters, friends died.
Never again will they hear their families say,
Happy birthday, good morning, nice day.

After many deaths, the word "vaccine"
now vibrates hope within our ear canals—
hope for normal times for the living.
If our ears truly had been humble,
we would not have complained;
we would gladly put on masks and
listening ears to bring back neighbors,
loved ones lost in the pandemic of 2020.

Creative Nonfiction
Matt Gregersen

Mount Josephine

We parked our cars in the trailhead lot and made our preparations, zipping granola bars and water bottles into bags, before setting off on the hike, six friends and two dogs, a sleek Weimaraner and dainty Lab. Friends since high school, the short span of years since graduation found us flung to different corners of the state. Yet we still made efforts to fit in a camping trip or two while Minnesota's milder seasons permitted.

Two days before, we had walked this same path. The hike that day started under speculative skies, with heavy clouds patrolling the blue above like marshmallow tanks. Weather is notoriously volatile on the North Shore. Anybody who has spent any time there knows that a clear sky can replace a thunderstorm before the last rain drop hits the ground. Being brash young men, we took the threat of impending thunder and lightning with a grain of salt.

Mount Josephine is a strenuous hike, beginning on a wide, flat, muddy path under a cooling shade of canopy, before turning drastically upward, rising six hundred feet in less than half a mile. At times the trail is remarkably straight, rising at an insistent incline into sparser tree coverage. Closer to the top, the trail becomes rockier, with switchbacks and miniature boulders to clamber over. It was here that the rains came.

It began as a gentle mist, but soon became stronger, the rain drops fattening as they fell. By the time we reached the summit, it was downright torrential. We stood on the bare rock and stared into an amorphous gray curtain enveloping us, and it took but a minute to be soaked to the bone. Being unable to stand under a tree to even light a cigarette, we began the way back down.

The path in some places was swollen with dirty gray rushing water. Navigating the slick rocks with a trembling dog between your ankles is no easy feat, but we all made it back down safely.

The volatile weather patterns proved true; as we changed into dry clothes at our cars and made the drive back to Grand Marais, the sun had emerged to shine on a wet and dripping world. And as we sat wearing waterlogged boots in Sven and Ole's, the floodgates opened again, and we watched shoppers on the street bolt for cover as the rain resumed and pounded the pavement.

If there is joy in novelty, then there is twice as much in familiarity. To know something well enough to experience it in a new way is to grow. The second time ascending Mount Josephine, our lungs and calves still burned. But muscle memory is a powerful thing, and our steps seemed twice as light. The dogs covered twice as much ground as necessary, running ahead, back, and ahead again the entire way.

We soon reached the peak once more, and were rewarded with a view unencumbered. Superior lay to the east, that wide throw of lustrous blue horizon. From the top of Josephine, the view is so dramatic as to be nearly disorienting. Waswagoning Bay circles to Pigeon Point, the Susie Islands, and far in the distance, Isle Royale appears as a hazy visage. Inland, the Superior National Forest rolls out of sight to the west.

We all found a spot to sprawl on the rocks and rest, talking and laughing, basking in the warm sun and cold wind that blew across the inland sea.

These trips and times happen less often now, perhaps an inevitability as we grow older. After a while, someone zipped up their backpack, someone crumpled up a granola bar wrapper, someone else screwed the cap on their water bottle. Nobody said a word; these cues were understood. We had made our climb, basked in the high summit, and descended with the sun and wind still in our minds.

Poetry
Susan McMillan

Astray
Soft drizzle in fall,
football game just into its second quarter
when we slipped out between bleachers
    crowded with locals.

My heart hopped with excitement of walking together
along the narrow uneven sidewalk, lights reflected
on every wet surface.

    It was innocence and awakening—
male hand never before wrapped around my own
as coarse denim of his blue jacket brushed my wrist,
thrill of not being with the group of friends I meant to be
    but instead

out on sodden streets of this ore-begotten town
lined with discreet old houses, whose windows
winked through the dark
    from behind their shadowed yards
where we slowed, then stopped.

He looked down, touched his lips to mine
and we shared a first kiss
    as streetlamp-sparkled beads of moisture
dripped from his shag of hair to cross my cheeks.

My coat was thin. We had no umbrella. Still,
    that dampness and cold never found me.

Poetry
Sharon Chmielarz

I Could Never Write a Poem to This
(after "I Could Never Write a Poem to This City," Alfredo Zaldivar)
May I sing with you, black cowboy
hat and buckle,

like your bass guitar
named Trouble Here and Gone,
Gone but Here,

like a match box on fire, rhythm
and tone aflame

like your knobbed and knolly
fingertips coaxing strings
to give it up,

like your left foot lives
by itself in the beat,

and your opened shirt
shows your throat to your chest
where your gold necklace rocks

to the clef in the cleft,
the chain, a pendulum

damp from your skin's
brown suede. Like your
song is not for possession,

your song,
not for my touching.

Creative Nonfiction
Donna Uphus

The Country House

The country house sat on a hill at the end of a long, weedy path that served as a driveway. Mom parked the car right in front of the sagging front porch. She just sat there in the driver's seat staring at the old house. "Are you kidding me?" she whispered to no one. I jumped out, climbed up the broken cement steps and walked back and forth on the porch, careful of the gaps in the floor boards. My heart beat wildly in my chest. I didn't care that the paint was chipped and cracked, that some of the window screens were torn, or that it was far away from the closest town. I loved that house from the very beginning.

I was nine years old when we moved to Minnesota and, while I lived in a lot of different houses in my short life, none was like the country house. No other houses stood right next to it.

When Mom finally got out of the car and opened the heavy wooden door, I flew past her into the big empty room. I twirled around on the worn wooden floor and dust rose up under my feet. The room had high ceilings and a window with a seat built beneath it. When I laid on it, I could see myself there on a lazy summer day reading a book. A big, black wood stove dominated one corner with a pipe reaching up the wall to the circle near the ceiling where it disappeared. Mom flung a window open and fresh air came rushing in.

I tore into the next room. Ah, the kitchen. The floor had ancient linoleum, gray with big pink flowers all over, with dark spots where chairs had slid in and out. I knelt down and touched the flowers; I thought it was beautiful. The painted cupboards along one wall were chipped and yellowed with age. A single light bulb hung from the ceiling and, when I pulled the string, it came to life.

When I lifted the handle of the red pumping thing by the dirty sink, brown, smelly water trickled out. The pump was a smaller version of the one by the back door at Grandma's house in South Dakota. I ran from the kitchen pinching my nose. Mom looked into the room and shook her head. "How do we get along without running water?" she asked as I brushed past her in silence.

The next room, I decided, was perfect for Mom's sewing stuff. It was sunny and warm with two long windows facing the old barn out back. Opposite the windows, a narrow staircase led to the second floor. The wooden steps creaked as I climbed up. At the top, the air was stuffy and hot and smelled like old shoes. Three doors revealed bedrooms. I claimed the one with fuzzy, swirly blue wallpaper for my own. I sat on the floor and imagined sleeping in that country house, in that very room.

My mother shouted that we should help bring stuff in just when Dad drove up with the moving van and it was official; we were moving in. I ran down and carried boxes of curtains inside, setting them down in the "sewing" room. Mom opened them up and she handed me some blue ones. I wondered how she knew that the room I chose was blue. I guess moms know those things without looking.

Mom and Dad didn't talk as we all hauled our stuff inside. I could tell Mom didn't love that country house, but when Dad winked at me, I knew he felt the same way I did about living there. We started to make it our home and I was happy.

Creative Nonfiction
Sharon Harris

Night Sounds

As an adult, I sleep restlessly.

My house has so many sounds, creaks, and soft thuds. When I had a cat, I was never concerned. Now I get spooked all the time and watch eerie shadows crawl and creep across my ceiling at night. I make sure my dog sleeps inside in the kitchen so I can blame her for the noises.

As a child, I slept on a screened-in porch with a feeble latch. Bats fluttered by outside and owls hooted. A buck would snort and crash through brush, a lynx would scream its hair-raising call from across the road. Coyotes yipped and howled in the back field. And a soft lapping sound told me a skunk was drinking from our kiddie pool beside the house.

I was a part of the night then. I drank in the fresh air, relished its cool caress, hoped for crashing thunder, and took all the sounds in stride.

As a child, I slept easily.

Poetry
Lane Henson

Walking to the Moon by Way of Lake Superior

The moon came tonight
to lead me down to the lakeshore.
That silvery-tongued siren—
    she's kept her promises before.

Her full face was framed by dark pine
boughs. I stood where Superior meets stone,
her reflection strewn like radiant ghosts
    across the water.

I longed to dispel
the old calcium of my bones
        slipped free of my shoes
    tested the shallows.

Her song was an open hymnal
at my feet, a song of minerals,
of the salt
    we must return to earth.

Each cold verse
    begged me to pursue.
Each wave's edge
    gleamed like a blade.

I could not turn back, friends.
I am walking to her still.

Fiction—Honorable Mention
Marlys Guimaraes

Crevices

Cassy hated to clean house. In fact, she figured out that she only vacuumed the bedroom carpet about four times a year. "Why bother? It's only for sleep," she'd say to herself when feeling guilty for her slovenly ways.

But every year or so, she went on a cleaning binge. With her long chestnut-colored hair pulled back into a ponytail, wearing an old pair of her navy blue nursing scrubs and beat up Nike's, she attacked dust, dirt, and debris with the passion she usually saved for the men in her life.

In past years, when she pulled off couch cushions to vacuum deep into the crevices, she'd find misplaced items, like Travis' pacifier that they looked hours for while he screamed, the lost keys to the tool shed padlock, and a gummy bear that was stuck so firmly to the upholstery she had to use a table knife to scrape it off.

This year was different. Yes, there were the usual ponytail holders, crumbled cookies, and such, but Cassy stopped short when she saw a sliver of black lace stuck deep into the back of the couch. She pulled on the lace to bring up a slender thong panty.

She hated thong underwear. When they were first married, Rich hinted she should give them a try, and she did, once. Then once again. Then never again. "Most uncomfortable piece of clothing I have ever worn," she told him.

Cassy held the wayward thong between her right thumb and forefinger, far away from her body. She plopped into the old blue recliner, having lost the heart for cleaning.

By the end of the week, she contacted a moving company and watched as furniture and household goods were loaded.

Rich returned from his business trip to an empty house. On the kitchen counter was an artist mat with a pair of black thong panties pinned to it like a butterfly specimen. The display was entitled—*Strike Three.*

Poetry
Pamela Wolters

A Coyote Night October 7, 2020
A coyote night of a melting moon
at the crest of a day of sun-tanned leaves
as Gulf Coast breezes venture north
and blue sky bowl overflows with gold.
Foggy dawns rise lazy and late
while blanketed lawns peek through calico leaves
driven by gusts from one driveway to the next,
up north where daylight retires with grace
like children obediently trudging to bed.
Descending dark summons wild gathered cries
at the dusk of a day of sun-tanned leaves
on a coyote night of a melting moon
molten gold of distant orb
round and big against a curtain of Autumn.

Fiction

M. E. Kopp

Super Nova

Nova waits outside the Qwik Trip. She leans between the bathroom doors, arms crossed, wet sweat on her T-shirt. The bright blue smell of glass cleaner punches through the stucco wall. Across the lot, perched on a pole twice as tall as Tasty's drive-through, a man-sized tub of cola screeches round and round

"You looking for something, hon?"

Nova licks her lips, tastes the bitter lipstick there. "Just waiting on my Dad," Nova says. She jerks her head towards the gas pumps.

The salmon-faced woman in the red apron, name tag Jodee, shrugs, goes back to scraping cigarette butts off the pavement and into a dustpan. A far-off motor unravels in the heat. The hum closes in. Pretty soon a pickup jumps the frontage road and plows into the lot. Jodee and Nova watch. A young man sidles out— shoulders like knobs, bones like blades beneath his shirt. He saunters close so Nova can see the two hairs dangled off his chin.

He thumbs his chest. "Dangerzone221. You RedNova?"

"Yep," Nova says. The cola cup squeaks out another rotation. Cicadas thrum in the weeds.

"Hop in." Dangerzone lopes back to the Nissan, all skirted in rust. Nova shakes off the Qwik Trip attendant's eyes. She climbs into the passenger side.

"Let's do this," Dangerzone says and grabs the clutch. Soon enough, Qwik Trip, the dilapidated Tasty's, and the rotating tub of cola drop away. Wind grazes Nova's ears and static unwinds from the radio. She tries not to think too far ahead of the tires, spinning faster than the posted twenty. They enter onto clean tar stretched between cornfields. Dangerzone settles in. His blue eyes cut her way.

"So . . . Nova, huh? Real name?"

"Yep." Nova scratches the arm where Father pinched her. Two purple crescents. The night she was born, he mistook a shooting star for a super nova. Could've been worse. She might've been

Comet. Asteroid.

"You sure you're sixteen?"

"Uh-huh." Thirteen-year-old Nova lifts her arm, checks the bruise in the side-view mirror. Sun flashes in its glass.

Dangerzone picks up the pace.

Now they're getting somewhere.

Aren't you tired of being scared? Marlene from CPS had said. Nova stared at the kitchen table. The ceiling fan ticked above them, spreading out flies. Finally, Marlene sighed. "Well. Call if he ever lays a hand on you." Maybe if Father hadn't been crouching in the basement, his remorse creeping up through the radiators and pimpling Nova's skin, maybe she would've felt less sorry for him and said something honest.

The Nissan crests a hill. Trees vanish. Pavement ends. Nothing but dirt road. Pasture either side. Before them a sheet of sparkling white that Nova realizes, as the truck tips forward, is Gull Lake.

"Wait. No," Nova says.

"Like a blaze of glory." Dangerzone jerks the shift between them. Wind beats around the cab. Sawgrass shrills around them. Gull Lake grows in the windshield.

"Stop," Nova screams.

Dangerzone pushes sixty. Dirt bursts beneath them. Ahead, a boat landing, water. Nova kicks the dashboard.

"No." She yanks the door handle. Suddenly she's back in that afternoon, when Mama stuffed jeans and T-shirts and Nova's plush animals into garbage bags, packed them in the Neon, rolled halfway down the drive. Nova pummeled the door until Mother pulled back up. They unpacked the clothes, and Father came home reeking of metal and grease. The deflated garbage bags lay like white skins on the floor. He stared around, then drove them to the Pizza Ranch, and no one said anything.

Dangerzone strains over the wheel, knuckles taut. Slime limns Nova's teeth. She knows the deal. No matter how much she screams, he's paid to keep going.

Tires hit water. Waves rush the windshield. Panic slams her chest. Everything bursts white.

Then a quiet. The engine cuts. The wind dies. The lake sloshes lazily against the tires. Dangerzone clicks on the wipers to smear dead moths away. The truck's nosed downwards on the concrete apron, bumper kissing water.

"Had you real scared there, huh?" Dangerzone says. Sweat slicks his arm and dangles in the scrum above his lip. He backs the truck up the boat launch, then guts it forward.

"You left nail marks on the dash." Dangerzone laughs. Nova shakes so hard she barely works the twenty from her pocket. Dangerzone keeps his eye on the road and tucks it in his own back pocket.

He drops her off at the Qwik Trip. The cola still squeaks around, but Jodee with the flapping dust pan's gone.

"So. Yeah. Tell your friends," Dangerzone says. The Nissan flaps away.

Nova walks home. She kicks up crickets. The first fireflies buzz about.

Tough shit, Marlene from CPS told Mother, who'd kept quiet, too. *Living that kind of fear, everyday, did something to a child.*

Did what?

Nova found Dangerzone online. People paid him for near-death experiences. *Can't do much for twenty,* he'd messaged her. *Whatever you can,* Nova wrote back.

Nova passes the mailbox. Sun glows gold in the windows. Maybe nobody's home.

But Father sat out on the porch, hiding in a blade of shade.

"Where ya been, my super Nova?" There's a smile in his sound. A cigarette in his fingers. The father Nova loves.

"Nowhere, Daddy." She leans her cheek on his arm, breathes his heat, thinks of waves crashing the windshield.

There ain't nothing he can do that'll scare her now.

Poetry
Susan McMillan

Headed Somewhere

Sun climbs through the window,
brings its own yellow blanket
to spread over your bed
    and spill onto the floor,

sweeps dust motes and bits of lint
    into its wide embrace,
where they pose, aloft in the spotlight
as you pass, bleary-eyed.

Sun slips a snail's pace along the rug,
reaches long legs beyond the door
and out across the hall, to rest big feet
right there on the stairway wall.

Head haloed in Sun's warm beam,
    you sit on the topmost step—
rumpled morning hairdo a haystack silhouette
time tows in its wagon
    toward something.

Fiction
Doug Lewandowski

The Empty Seat

The first time I met him was on the Randolph city bus. He was a foul-smelling, ill-tempered man who looked like he'd been around the block a few times and up and down the alley a lot more.

I was going to West St. Paul to the Mothers of Mercy Nursing Home as part of my Legion of Mary public service commitment during my ninth-grade year at the Catholic school I attended. I made the weekly trips there to visit Jimmy Doyle, a ninety-year-old retired carillon player. His last gig, before his stroke, had been at the National Cathedral in Washington, D.C.

When I got on the bus, there was nowhere to sit. It was crammed with students going home from high school. Kids stood in the aisles, holding tight to the hand rails, swaying back and forth as the vehicle careened down the street. I was tired and, spying an empty spot toward the back of bus, I staggered my way down the aisle, slipping between people to the unoccupied seat.

"Can I sit here?" I asked.

The old man raised rheumy eyes and replied, "Does it look like the damn thing's taken?" His breath radiated stale cigarettes made more pungent by a toothbrush-deficit topped off with a trace of gin. I sat down.

The bus continued to lurch down the potholed streets. Each pitch to and fro tipped me into the guy's shoulder. He grumbled and pulled into himself and wrapped a faded trench coat tighter around his rail-thin frame. My stop came and I got off.

The next week when I got on the bus, the seat was again empty next to the old man. I was tired from my Physical Training class, so I worked my way back and sat down next to him. "Hi," I said. He replied with a curt nod and stared out the window, pulling his coat snugly around his body.

Each week I got on the same bus and sat next to him. After several weeks I offered him a stick of Juicy Fruit gum in self defense against his aromas. He accepted. Every time after that he took the proffered gum.

One week he wasn't on the bus. The next week he was there. I handed him a stick of gum. He said, "Thanks."

"Nice day," I said.

He nodded his head.

"Didn't see you last week. You miss the bus?"

"No, I just had business," he said with a frown in an accented voice. We continued in silence.

The following week when I got on the bus, he looked up as I worked my way down the aisle. After the holy communion of the gum, he turned and said, "Where in the hell do you go every week?"

I explained to him about my visits with Jimmy. For the first time I saw a faint smile.

"I used to listen to bells a lot," he said.

"Really?" I said. "Where?"

"In Mons, in the Netherlands, at the Belfry."

"When were you there?"

He smiled a little more with a faraway look in his eyes. "A long time ago." He pulled his old coat around him and stared out the window and spoke no more.

The following week when I got on the bus, all the seats were filled, no sight of the old man. I had to stand. Week after week I looked for him, but he was never there. I stood all the time.

A month later as I was paging through a newspaper in the school library before leaving for Mothers of Mercy later in the day, there on the inside page was an obituary. The headline read, "Roland Murphy, Lover of Bells." I looked at the picture taken a long time ago and could see the shape of the man I'd sat next to on the bus all those times. He'd been a banker in Brussels, with family in New York who would miss him. I stared out the window at the overcast sky.

Later, as the bus went by the St. Paul Cathedral, the bells rang. I would miss Roland too. I pulled my school jacket tighter around me.

Poetry
Jennifer Jesseph

November Trees
bare of leaves
are forks
scraping a gray
blue plate.

Poetry
Deborah Rasmussen

Mother Tongue
Before this country
there was another.
Old they called it
as though no one
could recall its name
or where it was
except distant—
a week by ship
below decks
crowded with the sounds
of other Old Countries.

There was another tongue then,
the one I heard buried
in my elders' rough English,
the language of my roots.
It pulses in my genes

but who is left
to teach my lips old motions,
vowels, consonants, words
of that other place
that other life
too distant now
for me to re-
collect.

Creative Nonfiction
Ruth M. Schmidt-Baeumler

Process of Elimination

You entered the hospital. The first day they scanned for fever or coughing. It was a short, two-night stay with you drifting into eternal sleep. You were ready, I was ready, but the shock stopped my internal clock.

The time of your death was lucky for us—just before Corona closed down the rest of our lives in Germany. The funeral took place two days before lock-down. We hugged, cried, celebrated, shared stories and emotions freely. You would have loved it. Your daughter, her wife, and a niece played piano and sang for us. The pastor knew you well. Our granddaughters initiated a sing-along of "Holy Angels" as we exited the church. The flowers were just enough; they fit in the apartment and on the balconies. Your son built an eight-sided wood container for your ashes, which we will bury sometime in the future when we can dig safely together near the pink moccasin patch in Minnesota. Guests learned things about you they did not know. You were so present. At the reception we passed out packets of seeds with your name on them. I receive phone calls describing their growth. Each of us in our own Corona cell share the same sky, the clearer sunsets, the quiet streets, the personal grief.

Corona allows me to grieve behind closed doors. In public my mask hides my grimace and catches tears.

I spend my days with the bureaucratic nonsense of extracting your name from documents: bank accounts, deed to the apartment, clubs you socialized, church register. You disappear followed by a brief, "We're sorry for your loss," that sounds computer-generated. Corona messes with the process, prolongs the deletion of your name. Office workers are at home; everything has slowed down. I get impatient. I just want to get through this part. I want to get on with my life with you, not remove you from it.

Each utterance of "Please delete my husband from your register," doesn't make it easier, but the Pavlovian routine makes it less meaningful.

This elimination has a new vocabulary. There is not an instruction booklet explaining all I need to know. I am in a foreign country whose language I speak fluently, but this language of bureaucratic death legalese confounds me. I struggle because I do not want to learn it. You are not here to help me.

Poetry
Peggy Trojan

Air Mail
I smile to remember
our eyes meeting
across the room,
your finger casually
brushing your lip,
sending a kiss.

Poetry
Steven R. Vogel

Vine
The old vine grasped on the shed
is as ugly as anything could be,
a tangle of disorganized death
in dormancy that keeps
a rigid hope I yearn to possess.

But we are not alike in our wants,
for in a small time,
the wires of spring will pith him
well, leaking green as they go,
putting blotches back into places

they had abandoned with consent.
And so easily! A set of ornery
sticks made limber, blossoms
falling out like excess to paint
the green into a common miracle.

How glibly he spurns gravity
and all its benefits.
My eyes will fill with greed
to see it again like a taunt of year,
but one I cannot be without.

And the shears I steel to his nose
are but my love of hope,
my claim on his floating honey
when the air grows thick
with water and humming insects.

Poetry
Teri Joyce

Lines
Sheets hang on a line outside,
drying in the sun and the wind.

Words dry on my tongue and wind
out of my pen into lines.

The ink on my lines hasn't dried.
The tears in my eyes haven't dripped.

Wet sheets on the line drip
where my line cut through your mind.

Your lines cut through my heart
from the page I found on the deck.

I found your words on the deck,
too late to make mine unwind.

Too late to unwind my words.
Now you hang by a sheet on my line.

Creative Nonfiction—Honorable Mention
Pam Whitfield

People Say the Dumbest Things

My ankle required surgery last spring. I lay on my sofa in a cast for six weeks. As soon as the cast came off and the doctor said the word "rehab," I gathered up my kids and flew to the Carolinas to visit my kin. At that point, I just needed some good ole southern lovin' up.

I was pleasantly surprised by how well Delta accommodated disabled passengers. And the flight from Rochester to Atlanta was filled with Southerners, the real Deep South kind. "Awww, darling, just look at you," and "Bless yore little heart," followed me all the way to my seat—in the bulkhead row. Several men fought for the privilege of taking my crutches up front to the steward.

The first few days at my parents' house, I crutched my way around the neighborhood, in 95-degree heat, learning how to "walk at fifty percent weight-bearing" in an ugly black plastic boot. I kept my eyes glued to the pavement, not trusting my footing. My sister dressed me in a neon yellow reflective vest. She was right: I would never see a car coming,

Soon I could crutch and look up at the same time. Women waved at me; men nodded respectfully or raised one finger from the steering wheel. A gentleman backing out of his driveway called out, "I just want to know one thing: who won?"

"The surgeon," I told him. "He made a lot of money off this leg."

A leggy woman in her sixties stopped to tell me that she "walked up and down this road like you're doing—but with a walker—only two years ago. You keep it up, honey." Her words floated me and the plastic boot all the way home.

The next morning, a lady stopped in her station wagon. "I've been watching you go up and down this hill all week, darling," she told me. "If you need a rest, you just stop at my house. 2730.

Remember that." She didn't even tell me the name of her street: that's how well she knew my route. I found 2730 around the next corner, with a cute red rocking chair sitting on the front stoop.

The coup d'etat was the scooter man, who only exercised after dark. The first time he lapped me on my route, I put his age at fourteen. Who else would be out here, in a reflective vest and head lamp, whizzing by every five minutes, but a teenager too young to have his license?

Finally, he pulled up alongside me. "What happened to you?" he asked. I looked into his concerned face and saw a man well over seventy. Turned out he scooters every night because the doctor wants him to strengthen his right leg muscles. Bob knew my parents. He knew that my sister walked her yellow Lab in the evenings. He wanted to talk about the Mayo Clinic, who sent him a monthly newsletter, and the Cleveland Clinic, who did his sister's heart valves. He made me wish that I were ready for a scooter.

I felt well loved during my time of disability in North Carolina. But lest you think that I believe—erroneously—that Southerners are perfect, people did say ridiculous things to me too. We went to the beach and stayed in a high-rise. A drunk man in the crowded elevator was warned by his wife not to hit my leg. "I oughter hit it," he said, "so she'll remember why it's broken."

I wanted to say, "I oughter kick you, so you'll remember to listen to your wife," but my kids were with me and everyone else was giving me sympathetic "He ain't right" looks.

The following day, in the same elevator, another comedian said to me, "You oughta quit kicking people."

"I really should," I told him. "But people say the dumbest things."

Poetry
Phyllis Emmel

Writer's Blocks
I like to play with words
Stack them up
String them out
Turn them upside down
And backwards
I like to play with meaning
Up close and personal
Distant and cool
Warm and loving
I like to play with sound
Listen as it bounces off my tongue
And runs off to play with meaning
So why is it that sometimes
The words refuse to come out to play?
In the middle of the night
They dance across my mind
But fade at break of day
They stay inside my head
Afraid to meet the world
In the light of day

Poetry
Sharon Harris

After the Weekend
Sunday evenings
after a free-ranging weekend
are the hardest
nights to sleep

work tomorrow
rises ahead of me
like a wraith
while I yearn to slip away

the house noises
are louder than on other nights
the dog is more restless than usual
and whines from the kitchen

my mind shouts lists at me
things I must do tomorrow
my breathing is ragged and uneven
while I search for calm breaths to count

my legs twitch
and everything aches
there is no spot of comfort
on pillow or mattress

I cannot slow my whirring mind
I wait hopelessly for the day
to let me go and unravel
and let me drift away

Creative Nonfiction
Beth L. Voigt

Family Dinners

"What's for dinner?" was a reasonable question my daughters often asked when I picked them up from their after-school activities each night. I just didn't have an immediate answer. I sometimes developed my plans for dinner on the car ride home, and often times not until we entered the house and I was rummaging through the freezer to determine what was most expedient.

We ate as a family most nights, figuring if my parents could manage to corral nine of us kids around the table for meals three times a day for decades, I could manage it once a day for our family of four. But I simply didn't have the talent to put magnificent feasts on the table like Mom did.

Every day, three times a day, Mom cooked for our family of eleven and often other unexpected guests. I, on the other hand, filled two cereal bowls and was lucky to slice a banana on top as I hurried our daughters through breakfast and sent them off to school with bagged lunches.

In contrast, awaking early, still in her nightgown and robe, Mom stirred oatmeal, scrambled eggs, baked apples or flipped pancakes with, best of all, homemade vanilla syrup. Every noon hour, she served savory soup, grilled cheese sandwiches, or thick beef stew laden with vegetables when we walked in the door from school and then hurried back before the lunch recess bell rang.

Yet, these were only warm-ups to her greatest cooking feat of the day: Dinner. And it was there, as we sat around the kitchen or sometimes dining room table, that we feasted. She made herbed chicken roasting on a bed of seasoned rice, sour cream-laden beef stroganoff doused over thick egg noodles and white fish seasoned with thinly sliced onions and lemons.

Homework, athletic practices, music lessons, and any other

activities were considered less significant than family dinners. So, at six p.m., we were all seated at the table. And that's when the banquet was served. Mom, with the help of one or two of the older kids, presented three vegetables (often dill carrots, creamed peas, and pickled beets) as well as potatoes (sometimes mashed, sometimes baked, sometimes au gratin), meat (often beef but chicken or fish as well), and always salad and Jell-O with fruit.

The best I could manage for my family was a pot of spaghetti with marinara sauce or baked potatoes and chicken or, if I was lucky, some soup from my mom who made more than she needed some nights.

Despite ringing phones and doorbells, longing for forgotten salad dressing or a run to the bathroom, once we were seated, we stayed seated. The only exception was to get up to help Mom serve or clear away dishes. This was Mom's time to sit and visit with our family all at once, for the duration of a meal, uninterrupted. I think this may have been her favorite time of day.

It was my favorite time too, because everyone was welcome. Mom said we could always squeeze in another around the table. Whether we had one friend or five who we wanted to invite to dinner, we could. And it was then that I realized how lucky I was as my friends "ohhed" and "ahhed" at the array of choices and the delectable foods before us each evening.

I carried on this tradition as well, not because I expected any rave reviews from my daughters' friends but because I liked the dining room table surrounded by many conversations and much laughter—reminding me of growing up in a big family.

All know, I didn't inherit Mom's cooking talent nor culinary work ethic. When my children asked, "What's for dinner?" they often didn't wait for an answer and quickly followed it up with "Can we go to Grandma's house for dinner?"

Poetry
Micki Blenkush

Vacation Sunrise

Dark is the state in which we stride
down the boardwalk past the other hotels.
My daughter slows every few steps
to focus her camera into dawn's preshow.

At fourteen, she does not want me here
but needs me here, used the word *escort*
to ask me to set an alarm so she could make it
to the rocky inlet before the sun's 5:30 rise.

We're glad to see towers of rock
left standing by tourists the night before
as we arrive in time for her to capture orange
and pink streaking everything including us

and the gulls fanning the sky. Vacation birds
are novel birds and hence more picturesque.
Decades ago on this same beach, my husband
thwapped back to the hotel in flip flops

to grab our camera for a photo of Suess-like towers
stacked by a man who finally turned to tell us
that the trick is to simply listen. Today I feign
a distant gaze between sneaking photos

of my daughter who says *Would you stop*
but is now too busy lying shoulder to shore
aiming her lens into the waves
to notice the times I turn her way.

Poetry
Jennifer Hernandez

Open Borders
Tend your garden,
your little patch of land,
pull the weeds,
pray for rain,
cheer the seedlings
that they may grow into bounty.

May swarms of pollinators
feast at sweet blossoms.
May tiny feet clamber
across rich earth, when leaves
dry and drop. May joy spill out
in an overflow of abundance.

May I be a tourist
who visits this land,
no visa required,
gates open, benches ready
to receive those who would rest
and gaze upon the beauty.

There is no invasion here,
no swarms of pestilence
that spill across borders,
clamber over walls,
guards on high alert,
guns at the ready to stop
this imaginary plague.

Bees buzz in my garden,
pollinators. Without them
nothing grows.

Creative Nonfiction
Deb Schlueter

Silence

The first day of school was a scene from a horror movie—the bell rang to deserted hallways, lockers gaped half-open in silence, and motion-sensor lights turned off from disuse.

Surrounded by desks coated in dust and bulletin boards empty of life, I logged into each class. Icons appeared on a screen, pixels attempting to be students, their voices glitching from a strained internet, my students sitting on beds and kitchen chairs.

Kids tried—they really tried. But as the days wore on, frustration leaked into everything we did. Technology didn't work. Websites went down. Computers broke. "Sorry, you froze. Can you repeat that?" was copy-pasted into the chat room so many times I started to hate the phrase with a passion.

I asked, "How do you motivate kids to set down their phones and learn from miles away?" Nobody could answer my question.

Days dragged into weeks and months. Endless class periods that were both too long and too short. Few kids answered when I asked questions. Sometimes the ones that did had family screaming in the background.

There's only so much pressure you can set on twelve-year-olds before they break. Some disappeared for days at a time. Some logged into class and walked away from their computer. Others muted the "tab" and played a video game instead.

I couldn't blame them. There were many days I struggled with the fantasy that this was still school too.

I got a headache every day, talking to the nobody-icons that didn't respond. I rarely knew if they learned anything, or if I was wasting my time and effort. Sometimes I got enough assignments turned in that I thought most kids understood the concept. Often not.

"How do you stay inspired to teach, when all you can see are symbols pretending to be students?" I asked. "Am I doing this right?" The silence in response was loud in my ears.

Endless days blurred into each other, worrying about students I wouldn't recognize if I passed them in the store. Were they warm enough? With enough food? Safe and healthy?

It was an epic tug-of-war, with the students and me in the middle. "Don't give any kids failing grades, have patience, we'll deal with it when this pandemic is over," pulling against "Start picking up the pace, get through your standards, don't let the kids fall too far behind because there's generational damage happening in front of your eyes."

After nearly a year of loneliness and staring at computers, two dozen students crammed back into my classroom. It was both an awesome return to normalcy and oddly unnerving, the "keep away" mantra crashing headlong into preteens desperate for attention.

A month back, too many kids still huddle deep inside sweatshirts, hoods pulled over their heads, silent shadows of who they were. Too many have forgotten how to act around other people. Too many are addicted to phones and vapes and worse. Too many now scribble "School Sux" all over their notebooks. It's becoming obvious that no matter how hard we tried, there are huge learning gaps.

Even though masks block smiles and social distancing rules make school awkward, a slow rebuilding process needs to begin. "Start reteaching social skills, focus on their emotional well-being, and begin working to get their academics caught up," I was told by the people who know best.

"How do I do all that?" I ask them.

I'm still waiting for something other than silence.

Poetry
Georgia A. Greeley

Fumble Days

If the dish could fall off
the counter, it will.
The tape will fold in on itself.
Keys will fall through my fingers,
through the decking floor boards,
and land in the mud.
My pocket will catch on the
door latch and rip
while I'm hurrying to my meeting
only to find
I read the clock wrong;
I'm an hour early.

I should have figured it out when I fell out of bed,
and just climbed back in . . .

Poetry
Marsh Muirhead

Visiting First Lutheran
Asked to share the peace,
I loosen my tie,
trying to pass
this awkward moment
in finding some comfort
for myself, both hands
too busy with this knot
around my neck
to reach out
to some stranger's
open arms
while I try to find
a way out of this.

Creative Nonfiction
Sara Sha

How Good Customer Service Can Save the World

Once upon a time, we needed each other to flip through various tasks in our lives. We needed human interaction to make a phone call, to buy a bag of flour. We had human interaction when filling our gas tank or getting directions or buying a sweater. Now we do these things on our own.

Self check-out lanes, online shopping, online banking, all scream self-reliance and convenience, but each situation takes us step-by-convenient-step away from each other. Increased self-reliance means we can develop a hard shell of self-sufficiency and needing someone else is an aberration or even an annoyance. Sometimes we blur the line between human and machine, using this human to get what we need, then move on, or on the other side of the counter, meeting this human's need so we can go on to the next one, the next one, until the line is gone and we can retreat into our castle and pull up the draw bridge.

Working in customer service has been fascinating for me. You intersect one individual who carries the weight and worries and joys that have accumulated in their day and their life so far with another person who carries the weights and worries and joys that have accumulated in their day and their life so far for one teeny segment of the day. And that interaction can change the energy for either person for hours, sometimes days.

I remember having to pick up a gift card at a restaurant. Simple task. Request card, pay for card, leave. Cross it off my mental to-do list and move on to my next task. So I go into the restaurant, barely making eye contact with the guy at the register.

But.

This guy. He didn't do anything extraordinary, but he was funny and engaging enough that it surprised me and I was laughing out loud as I went back to my car. In addition to checking this off my mental to-do list, I also noticed the color of the sky and the person getting out of their car next to mine. I smiled at them; they smiled back.

The stories of bad customer service get a lot of attention and people relish righteous indignation through yelling, complaining to others, leaving scathing online reviews.

But then there are the good stories that don't often get shared. The time a clerk surprised you with a pun, the time an issue was resolved cheerfully and relief was felt all around, how inexplicably a person told you the very words you needed to hear as they handed you your receipt.

These teeny joyful interactions are like colorful shining beads on a string, leaving people laughing in parking lots and smiling at strangers. When the big relationships of our lives are blowing up in our faces, these small interactions remind us of our worth.

Having worked in customer service, I also realize it's not just up to me to make the magic happen; it requires participation from the customer. I can be as warm and joy-giving as I can be, but if a customer approaches me like I'm a machine, the interaction is flat, cold, lifeless. But simple eye contact and a thank you can help both of us see each other. Hello, human being. I see you. Here's a bead.

I don't think it's a long shot to imagine that if we spent our days exchanging beads, our accumulations of yards and ropes of colorful shining beads would prettify our days, liven our hearts, and open our eyes to the wonder of human connection, even for a brief exchange. And I don't think it's a long shot to imagine that if we all walked around drenched in beads, with beads so plentiful they bounced on roads and sidewalks and skittered across windshields and scattered at our feet, the world would be a better place.

Poetry
Sue Bruns

A Comet's Shadow
Searching for signs of the comet, I
drive to the south bay boat landing.
Beside me my Shadow sits, wondering
Why, tonight, did she rate a front seat ride?
She fixes her brown eyes on me. I
pat her head, cradle her muzzle.
This evening is special, I tell her. We're
hunting, tonight, for a comet! She
lowers herself on the rug-covered
seat while I search the night sky for a
glimmering streak somewhere below
the Big Dipper's bowl.

We watch (I watch),
she waits, we leave.
I drive, I search,
we wait, we leave.
The pattern repeats.
I see no comet,
billions of years old,
no fuzzy star with
the hint of a tail.

I've brought no telescope, no binoculars with me.
How many more once-in-a lifetime events
will I miss due to lack of an adequate plan?
NEOWISE won't return for 68 centuries.

My Shadow doesn't mind. She got a front seat ride.

Poetry—Honorable Mention
Amy C. Rea

Phone Call
When the nurse called,
the nurse with neon-pink
hair gashed irregularly
around her head,
tats trickling down
the back of her neck,
pierced ears, nose, tongue,
who tried so hard—
and failed—
to keep a neutral face
while changing Dad's IV
as the man in the room next door
bellowed, "I'm done,
Goddamnit, I'm done!"
from his bathroom,
the nurse who looked
the other way when I
smuggled in beer,
then said, "If he can't have
a Corona now, then when?"
and laughed when I offered her
one too and said she had
a fully stocked fridge at home,
who laughed easily, teased
Dad about his fondness
for the Andrews Sisters,
when she called and said,
in a monotone, as if reading a script,
"Your father has entered
the final stage
of his hospice journey,"
I knew it was hard
for her
too.

Creative Nonfiction—Honorable Mention
Bernadette Hondl Thomasy

Movie Money

In the 1950s, money was tight for our farm family of five. We economized in ways big and small. Instead of owning a sedan, we made do with a pickup truck that could haul cattle feed and straw bales as well as transport the family. We did without indoor plumbing, making cold, nasty treks to the outhouse in the winter. In the kitchen, we cooked primarily with home-grown foods and economized by using half the amount of expensive, store-bought items, like nuts, chocolate chips, or raisins. Hand-churning butter in a jar, canning and freezing garden produce, making noodles and cakes with broken eggs that couldn't be sold—all kept food costs down.

Family entertainment, of course, was considered a luxury item. Our family did not own a television set. We pre-teen daughters relied on the radio to fuel our imaginations. Programs such as *The Lone Ranger, Our Miss Brooks,* and *Our Gal Sunday* fostered an obsessive desire for drama—one that could only be satisfied by going to the movies in our hometown, nine miles away.

Owatonna had two theaters: the Roxy, an older, not-very-clean place, and the State Theater, an up-to-date venue that showed the latest films. Our choice, the Roxy, was cheaper: admission was twelve cents for kids and fifty cents for adults. If my older sister and I could find $1.24 in change around the house, the family could go to the movies. That was before our baby sister needed a ticket.

The first place to search for change was Dad's overall pockets. We emptied them on the floor hoping to find a few coins in the mess of oats, corn kernels, washers, bits of hay and straw. Next, we looked in the basement near the washing machine where we had previously emptied pockets and may have forgotten to bring coins up to the kitchen. Then there was Mom's purse. She didn't mind if we collected some loose dimes or nickels floating on the bottom. Her coat and pants pockets also were fair game in our hunt. Returning empty pop or beer bottles could also yield movie money, but that took planning and a trip to a nearby country store to collect the refunds.

When we did scrounge up the $1.24, we girls were entranced during the coveted two hours in a dark, cozy theater. We didn't even mind not stopping at the concession stand; the smell of freshly popped corn was good enough. We settled in. First a news reel. Then a *Looney Toons* cartoon got us laughing and primed for the feature. We delighted in family comedies with Lucille Ball and many Westerns, our Dad's favorite, like *Hondo* with John Wayne and *High Noon* starring Gary Cooper.

The power of the big screen lingered with us for weeks— snow-topped mountain vistas, colorful period costumes, a passionate kiss, emotional theme music from the final scene. Then on the next rainy or cold Sunday afternoon, when we could not work outdoors, the urge returned. Hollywood called; we had to see a movie. The hunt began again. For $1.24 in change—movie money.

Poetry

T. S. Baxter

My Civic Duty, Or, How I Get Around
Jolts from the cracked roads
make the windshield wipers go
& pot holes cause the radio's
knob to pop on.
C'mon, Honda. Don't you know
I'm ignoring the news again today?
Regardless, I scarcely hear it
under the rumbling muffler
& the axles that squeal
with every wrench of the steering wheel
that disintegrates into plastic flakes
& sticks to my fingers like fish scales.
I pull the "automatic" window up by hand
& ignore the dashboard warnings (Check Engine, Low Battery),
focusing on the windshield chip,
promising myself it's not spreading.
Every other payday, when rent isn't due,
Babe & I weigh repairing
a torn boot against shot shocks,
a seeping oil pan against leaking rack & pinion,
an exhaust patch against an axle shaft assembly,
alignment adjustments against a coolant flush,
new tires against tie rod ends.
& it all costs forty times more than what the car's worth.
Our year's entire savings was decimated
by a timing belt replacement.
I keep paying to keep the car working,
so I can keep working,
so I can pay to keep the car working.

Poetry
Charles Kausalik-Boe

The Repairman
Your eyes, dark and quiet, peeking out
above your mask, tell me it's been a long day.
Your black hair sticking out from your stocking cap
like straw on the scarecrow.
Your body moves with determination
under your shirt with your name
sewn above your left breast pocket.
You broke the ice off the dam with
your bare hands,
a stronger, better man than me.
Your eyes, hair, hands, body
awaken feelings I have not felt for years.
Young enough to be my son,
I hold my thoughts,
I suppress my feelings.
I am modest, afraid.
Yet, I feel and dream imagining
life among the stars.
The world plays with me
as I watch your back
while stirring a boiling pot.

Creative Nonfiction
L. E. Newsom

My Doctor's Advice

"You are carrying too much weight around, dear," he said gently, as if I could set it down and just walk away from it. He tried to be discreet, but I noticed he changed one of my health diagnoses from "overweight" to "obese."

Don't get me wrong. I am all for some anti-couch-potato moves. I enjoy getting into the gym pool if it is as warm as bath water. I'll even do a few exercises up against the pool wall. However, when I surface, I have been mistaken for a baby beluga coming up for air.

But I made myself stay in the pool for an hour, moving the entire time, an immense change of pace for me. The clock on the wall moved so slow, I was certain the battery had died a quiet death just as I had entered the pool. People who came to swim laps, came and went, as I watched the movement of the sun through the large windows, coming closer to the horizon.

Finally, I made my way back to the locker room. The shower area reminds me of junior high gym class where one had to figure out how to shower without anybody looking at your stage of puberty. It is easier here because you can leave your swim suit on and you don't have a gym teacher belittling you.

Entering the carpeted locker area, I am dripping all over the floor. With each falling drop of water, I notice the increased odor, somewhere between a pile of used jock straps and rotten eggs.

The bench that I have taken a seat on is a large piece of granite. I try to keep myself discreetly covered as I struggle with my clothes clinging to my damp body. I take inventory of the differences since junior high.

I never was one who could go braless. Any quick movement would result in bilateral black eyes. The term pendulous was always appropriate, but now they spend their time pointing toward my shoes unless I cinch them up tightly. My abdomen shows a wide scar from the tip of my nose to the edge of my pubic hair from being filleted in an operating room a few years ago. The scar from the gallbladder removal bisects the vertical scar with a deep punch in the end where the drain was placed. The stretch marks from my pregnancies, although lightened in color, are still present. The rolls of my abdomen are usually covered by my loose tops. I may have gained a few pounds, but I have always been a big girl. I haven't changed *that much.*

I struggle with my cotton panties as they roll into a bunch when I try to pull them up and keep my towel in place. Abruptly, the door from the shower room pops open and in steps a young girl about twenty. *She is stark naked except for her flip flops.* She heads for a locker near mine in search of some forgotten shower item.

I discreetly observe her stage of puberty. Her chiseled butt is firm, her long legs sculpted. Her breasts are soft mounds pointing forward all of their own accord. Her nipples are firm and erect. She appears to have never been belittled by a gym teacher.

Silently, I hope a part of her anatomy gets caught in the latching mechanism as she slams the locker door shut.

Poetry
Cheryl Weibye Wilke

January
I still remember
as a child the after-

school afternoons
offering their lessons

in finger-nipping cold
and tales about

the thieves of early winter
who minute-
by-minute steal away

the frost-laden daytime hours. But,

I remember, too, sitting
on Grandma's sofa—

a dark jungle
velvet with rain forest wild,
dancing ferns and fronds—

facing the west, and
looking up in disbelief,

at the miracle
of warmth and light

streaming through
a basement window.

Light so much brighter
against the darkness.

Poetry
Meridel Kahl

Darkhouse Fishing
You open the door
remove the century-old spear
from its hook on the wall
unfold two camp stools
inches away from the hole
augured in the ice this morning.

You tie a string to the decoy,
a white wooden fish
with red markings
on its head and fins.
You glide, then dart it
through blue-green water
suffused with light.
We wait with easy patience
inside these dark walls
for a fish that never appears.

We sit together
wrapped in the quiet
of our own thoughts,
watch the glow of a February sun
held in the bowl of the lake,
grateful for silent depths
of winter water.

Fiction
Jennifer Hernandez

Firecracker

Firecrackers startled me awake. That or gunshots. But firecrackers were more likely seeing as how it was the 5th of July and there hadn't been any gunshots in our neighborhood since Vernon Stadtler's kids moved him into the Memory Care unit at Whispering Oaks. Reluctant to leave my cozy nest of sheets, I blinked a couple of times to clear the fog and had just started going over my mental to-do list for the day, when it washed over me. Great Aunt Beverly. Firecracker red lipstick and nail polish to match. She was the only one of my grandmother's sisters who had painted her nails. They'd all grown up on a farm in North Dakota and such things were suspect. But Aunt Bev had always been a looker, and even when she was in the nursing home, she had kept up her weekly manicure appointments.

Aunt Bev had been gone for ten years today. She went suddenly. Her heart. I always remembered the date because I'd met my husband the night before she died, at a 4th of July picnic hosted by my grad school roommate's musician boyfriend. The evening had ended with a backyard bonfire, several long-haired boys with acoustic guitars, and more bottles of Leinenkugel than was probably wise.

One of the long-haired boys—now neither long-haired nor a boy—stuck his head in the bedroom and said, "I'm going for a run. My mom called. She said the kids are fine. She's taking them to the park, and she'll bring them home after lunch."

"Bless that woman," I said. From the amount of light coming in from under the blinds, I could tell that this was the latest I'd slept in months. Since the last time my mother-in-law had kept the kids overnight.

The screen door banged shut as my husband left for his run. I peeled myself out of bed, threw on some shorts and a tank top, and tied my hair back into a ponytail. I glanced into the mirror, studiously avoiding the grays threading their way through the brown of my shoulder-length bob. When was the last time I'd been in for a trim? Did I have time for that before the kids got home? Did I care to enough to bother?

I poured a cup of coffee and let my mind wander back to Aunt Bev and the syrupy pink Shirley Temples she'd always served my sister Trish and me when we visited her townhome, the maraschino cherries carefully plucked from a jar in her pristine refrigerator. Aunt Bev never had any kids of her own, so she doted first on our mother and later on Trish and me.

Eyeing my callused heels and naked toenails, I made a snap decision. I was going in for a pedicure. Forget the to-do list. Aunt Bev would approve. I slipped into a pair of flip flops, refilled my coffee, and climbed into the car.

A few blocks down the street, I spied a large neon yellow tag board poster planted on the corner lot next to the stop sign. YARD SALE. 2 BLKS, GO LEFT. So I did. The sale was easy to find. Clothes racks, card tables, and old furniture covered the yard. I couldn't understand what had gotten into me. I wasn't normally an impulsive person. It must have been the unexpected freedom of being alone—no kids, no husband. I had forgotten what it felt like to have so much control over my own time.

I parked my car along the curb and got out. At the first card table, I paused reverently at the piles of paperbacks from my youth —Stephen King, Danielle Steel, James Michener. These were the paperbacks passed back and forth among the female relatives of my family. Aunt Bev had been partial to Danielle Steel.

Then an item on the next table caught my attention. A white patent leather handbag with a silver clasp. Just like the one that Aunt Bev had carried on our trips to West Acres Shopping Center, where we would try perfume and make-up samples at the Dayton's cosmetics counter, then stop for a cone at Baskin-Robbins— peppermint candy for me and butter pecan for her. I walked over to the handbag and opened the clasp, revealing the faded turquoise satin lining inside. I lifted the bag to my face and breathed deeply. Jean Naté and wintergreen Lifesavers. Whether the smells actually came from the handbag or from my memory was immaterial. I gladly paid $2 for the handbag and plunked down two quarters for a couple of Danielle Steels for good measure.

Back in my car, I checked my watch and found that I had just enough time for a pedicure and a quiet lunch of anything but mac and cheese before my mother-in-law delivered my kids back to the house. I patted the patent leather handbag on the passenger seat and smiled. Usually, I carried a diaper bag instead of a purse, and my recent reading choices tended toward *Chicka Chicka Boom Boom* and *No, David* rather than anything with actual chapters.

The kids were going to love my pedicure, I decided. My daughter wants to be a fire fighter when she grows up. Red has always been her favorite color.

Poetry
Vincent O'Connor

The Geometry of Insomnia
Unable to sleep,
I watch my love on
her back,

breath so shallow
the covers scarcely move.

As gentle snores decamp from
her aquiline nose,

instead of counting
sheep,
I work to calculate
the hypotenuse
of its prominent bridge.

Poetry
Lina Belar

Pandemic

Like a ship crossing the ocean, much can happen
Between the once familiar shore and the unknown.
There could be shipwrecks or harsh storms.
Days of feeling becalmed. Memories can fade,
As well as the once clear vision of the future.
When a ship is blown off course, new maps must be redrawn.
The longer I am at sea, the harder it is to imagine
Firm ground and the more I long for the land I left behind.

Poetry
Yvonne Pearson

All Morning the Snow
All morning the snow fell as feathers
floating to the ground, a gentle envelope

for our pandemic-wearied minds,
inducing a silence, a rest we have earned

by our patience, by forced absence of action.
The snow outlines the trees with a coat

of erstwhile ermine, only warmth the beauty.
Some days the trees object, rock in the wind

until they are barebacked and free once again.
Some days the snow hardens to ice, paves the walks,

a fierce lockdown fitting this world
that has taken choice away from us.

Before this lassitude, before this pandemic-wearied,
war-wearied, cruelty-wearied year, long before

this body wearied with age, new snow would raise breath
like wings in my chest, bear a vision of a new world.

Flurries would spiral, frolic and gambol,
summon our spirits to spheres unseen.

In this brutish year, cloaked among the quieting flow,
in the settling silence of snow, when I can gaze

at the interstice between the flakes, I gain a glimpse
of the vibrant, gamboling world I once knew.

Fiction
Ryan M. Neely

Testify!

They say we read books to experience the world through other people's eyes.

To prepare us for the what-ifs—the possible dangers—of our own lives.

Like a child being born with a learning disorder.

Or the gradual, life-sapping onset of ALS.

Or cradling your wife's crumpled body after a hit and run and lying to her that everything will be okay.

Sometimes, though, books don't really cover everything. Sometimes it's important to imagine the worst. Just in case.

Maybe you imagine moving to a tropical island after the accident. Becoming a beach bum.

Maybe you imagine filling a backpack with a handful of clothes. You leave behind your house. Your car. Your friends and family. All to trek into the wilderness where you teach yourself to live off the land, or to jump on a train and end up in New York. Anonymous. Where nobody can remind you of her.

Maybe you work your way through a thousand women, leaving a heartbroken trail of disappointment and hate. Because none of them could possibly live up to who she was.

But the moment you truly understand that she's gone, none of that imagining counts for shit.

Instead you spend the first few months imagining new things.

Like what it would be like to step in front of a bus or to chew on the barrel of a revolver. Anything just to see her again.

And all the while you're having to face reality. Like how you have to cure and dry cast iron instead of letting it soak and rust. Or how polypropylene shreds or shrinks if it goes in the dryer. Or how all those meals she cooked on all those nights after a long day at work took so much longer and tasted so much better than a

Styrofoam cup of noodles.

Then, when the ragged edges of life start to weave themselves back together and the most tragic thing you ever thought you would experience is over and done with . . . well, you start to imagine new things.

Like maybe how the trauma of having to throw out clothes, crusted stiff with crimson and plastered to your body with the same blood that had welded shut one of her eyes and frozen solid to her scalp in the snow, how maybe that trauma had blocked out the memory of a license plate.

A memory that comes back as slow as normal life: the picture of a loon and the numbers 446.

Like maybe how, rather than dinner and a movie like you used to do, you might decide to spend your evenings parked at the same corner. Your lights off, but the engine running for heat. Nothing but silence in the car so you can concentrate. So you can search for the Olive Drab 4Runner with a small dent in its front quarter panel.

Maybe your imagination would run wild then.

Maybe you'd imagine spotting the SUV after months of waiting. Imagine following up the highway out of town. Keeping a good quarter mile back. Your lights off. Memorizing the back end. The whole license plate, 6F446.

Maybe you'd imagine cruising past the driveway. Making a U-turn a half-mile down the road. Parking in the ditch of a nearby service road. Maybe, in your imagination, you'd hope the crisp, frozen air, the cozy aroma of woodsmoke, maybe they'd bring you back to your senses.

But this is your imagination where anything could happen.

So, maybe you creep through the woods. Stick to the shadows to cross the lawn. Peer into a darkened window. Maybe that's where you see him. Through the living room and into the kitchen, lit up like an Independence Day Carnival. Maybe he's packing food down his gullet like his throat is an old muzzle loader. His knee tapping Morse Code under the table. Frantic. Frenetic.

Maybe there's a woman at the table across from him. Glasses and bangs and a sparkling smile. Her mouth forming the words, "What's going on with you lately?"

Maybe it's the way she looks at him. Worried. Loving. With a hint of hope for the future. And maybe it's the way he looks at her in return. Annoyed. Angry. Afraid.

Maybe the way he seems unworthy of her—this creature who so resembles everything you'll never have again—maybe that's how your imagination justifies going in through the back door. Grabbing the nine iron from the bag in the hallway and the carving knife from the counter.

Maybe that's what made it okay to swing the club into his ribs. His knees. His ankles.

Maybe your imagination reminds you that death is too easy for him. Too painless.

Maybe that's why you imagined subduing the woman. Tying them together. Face to face. Waiting for him to regain consciousness so you could show him what it was like.

Make him watch the life drain from her face. Her smile droop into despondency. Her loving worry shift to beseeching terror and then to nothingness.

Maybe you imagine leaving him this way. Trussed up. Drenched in her life. With nothing but a long, empty road ahead of him.

But even you couldn't do that to another human. It would be too cruel.

The twelve of you are here to pass judgment. Ask yourselves, of all the things you imagined, did you experience the truth?

Poetry
Kathryn Knudson

Conversion—1989
More than once, setting the table
for Sunday dinner after church,
my mother would mumble
Lutherans could depress an angel.

Shortly after Easter she snapped.

As the children's choir, all rustling
dresses and squeaky patent leather,
filed back to smiling parents, she
started to clap. Loudly. Defiantly.

Hesitantly, others joined.

Before long the congregation
applauded after every performance:
the adult choir, the bell choir, the
fifth-grade alto saxophone quartet.

Poetry
Nicole Borg

Cousins

At your house, our moms would style
their hair, curl their eyelashes, walk through
a perfume haze, leave us for a couple of hours.

We would ride the wooden banister
by the front door. Run screaming
through the house playing *Wizard of Oz*—
I wanted to be a princess so I had the slippers,
Kelly cackling on the broom, Sheila
the one who got her front tooth chipped.
Some nights, you boys did magic tricks
from the David Copperfield box.

We built a haunted house
nailing blankets to the walls of the rental,
Kelly hid in the sofa sleeper under the cushions
so he could rise up from the dead.
Is it wrong I don't remember your voice?
I remember Loren's absence of voice,
even when we were playing, even
when we were having fun, he barely spoke.

You were the oldest, a teen already,
places you wanted to be. I saw
your shadow beneath the old tree
with the tire lolling at the end of the rope.
That Christmas you got the cheap-metal
hockey game, laid it out in front of the TV.
You crouched over it, your fingers
pulling triggers, your face concealed.

And now, one last magic trick.
You make yourself disappear.

Poetry
Mary A. Conrad

Linguistic love
like noisy train cars rattling
across aging trestle tracks
the peculiar sounds of Spanish
flap and lisp and hiss
against my awkward tongue
scouring decades of rust off
neural pathways that once gargled
my French "r" and pursed my lips
around the German "ue" and "oe"

next winter an Iberian jet
will drop its landing wheels and
touch down on a runway in Malaga
redeeming tortured memories
of pretzeled tongue-twisting
and vocabulary flash-carding
in this lonely time of COVID
like birth and new life transform
past labor pains into awe and delight

for my granddaughter, her mom
and me—three generations
of foreign language aficionadas—
planning this Andalucian getaway
seals our pledge to polish accents
and let budding fluency bloom
among native speakers basking
in Mediterranean sunshine
along the famed Costa del Sol

Creative Nonfiction
Niomi Rohn Phillips

Equal Rights

I wasn't surprised when Granddaughter Katie asked me how to make broth for spaetzle soup. After Thanksgiving dinner, she had foil-wrapped the turkey carcass and had taken it to the Minneapolis apartment she shares with a boyfriend. They cook together. They also read the same books. And they camp and hike. Last winter when they visited us in Hawaii, they braved the treacherous mountain Kalalau trail.

When Katie was a little girl, I gave her my Equal Rights Amendment bracelet. It took. She marched for George Floyd in my stead and grieved with me for Ginsburg. She's my beta reader and the keeper of my novel in case of flood, fire, or computer crash.

She shares my ancient passions. I'm grateful but despairing—it has been *fifty years* from my ERA fight to the election of Kamala Harris. And we're still fighting for the right to abortion? And for adequate childcare? And equal pay?

Mine was the generation of hope and excitement. We had fire in our bellies. Anything was possible. Inspired by Frieden, emboldened by women like Steinem, we infiltrated local school boards and county commissions, ran for public office. But like "Old Paint," we are heading west.

Katie is my fulfillment. An everything woman. She makes soup. She reads. She's politically active. But her fight is intense rather than exhilarating. I'm sad for the lost joy in the quest for equal rights. I do envy her sexual freedom. For that, we virgin brides *wish that we were young and foolish again.*

Poetry—Editor's Choice
Meridel Kahl

Autumn 2020
We sat outside
in lawn chairs
on benches
at picnic tables,
shared our lives across six-foot divides.

Days shortened—
we lingered past dark.
Unwilling to give in to the cold,
we brought mittens, hats, extra coats, blankets.

We watched September gardens die
October leaves turn.
We closed our eyes
to November's naked trees,
asked the lengthening shadows,
Is this the last time
until next summer?

In December we came inside
warmed ourselves
with pots of steaming soup
thick socks, fleece robes
quiet times by the fire.

We shivered, chilled
by the absence of each other.

Poetry
Joni Norby

Julie
Floating above all else,
aloof and distant,
deep and deeper you
go into yourself.
Like all present things,
you cannot stay.
Away, away you settle
into that blue-patterned room
with the perfect view.
Can I meet you there?
Can I be with you?

Poetry
Mary Scully Whitaker

Harmony
Let us not sing in unison
Let us sing in harmony
creating a richness
blending differences

Let us sing in harmony
listening to each other
blending differences
in the fullness of song

Listening to each other
each a separate strong voice
in the fullness of song
we come together

Each a separate strong voice
creating a richness
we come together
Let us not sing in unison

Creative Nonfiction
Audrey Kletscher Helbling

Minnesota Mardi Gras 2021

I scroll through the Facebook photos looking for my eighty-eight-year-old mom. But she's not among images of Parkview residents celebrating Mardi Gras. I want to find her, to see a smile curving her mouth below the oxygen tubes that clip her nostrils.

A year has passed since I walked through the front doors of her southwestern Minnesota care center and into her room. A year since I kissed Mom's cheek, hugged her, stroked her hand, sat on the edge of her bed while a machine pumped oxygen into her lungs. COVID-19 restrictions kept us apart, although I visited her in late June through a window while a staffer held a phone and repeated everything I said. Mom doesn't understand how to use a phone.

I bought her a bouquet of garden-fresh flowers from the Faribault Farmers' Market and a *Curious George* children's book during the summer visit. She's developed an affection for The Man in the Yellow Hat and his mischievous monkey. She laughs at their antics flicking across the TV screen in the room she calls home. I don't understand the connection. But, if a man and a monkey make her happy, then I'm happy.

When I view those Mardi Gras photos, minus Mom, I see the happiness of other residents. Smiles below bright eye masks decorated with feathers. Smiles above colorful beads draped around necks. Jaunty smiles below prop hats. If not for the face masks on staffers, I might think the pandemic had ended. But those photos and the daily case and death numbers from the Minnesota Department of Health tell me otherwise. There have been cases in Mom's long-term care facility, the official lingo for a place I'd prefer tagged with a homier moniker. But no deaths.

And now, a year into this pandemic, the Parkview family is celebrating Mardi Gras in a community of mostly Norwegians.

163

Certainly not French. But who cares? Perhaps those of Norse descent secretly prefer swamp punch, muffuletta sliders, and bananas foster to lefse and lutefisk.

Some 1,270 miles from New Orleans, these seniors are rediscovering joy. A reason to smile. A reason to connect, to laugh, to embrace life. Even if my mom wasn't at that party, I expect she's smiling, too, maybe even laughing at a playful monkey on her TV screen. And 120 miles away, I'm scrolling through the Parkview Facebook page, from my Minnesota city of French heritage, hoping for a glimpse of the mom I love. And miss.

Poetry
Jan Chronister

Watercolor Hero
When I was a young wife
I went for months
without thinking of my mom.
Now I remember
how she stayed in the shade,
never learned to ride a bike
or swim. She packed
my dad's lunch each morning
in a paper bag with his name on it,
had supper on the table at 5:30
Monday through Friday.
Cooking, scrubbing, laundry
all done with no complaints,
every holiday a splash of bright colors
in her washed-out world.

Poetry
Kathryn Knudson

The Minutiae of Fingerprints

The City of Hartland is a village, one
of many spaced six miles apart on the
railroad line running north to Minneapolis,
disappearing past Des Moines.

Hartland expanded, as railroad towns did,
then contracted, as railroad towns did.
The railroad lost favor to the highway.
The highway lost favor to the interstate

ten miles east, out of sight, beyond hearing.
Today a freeway exit sign marks Hartland's
presence which is more than most towns of
three hundred receive as if the world isn't

only literally passing them by but denying
their existence. These rural communities
may appear insignificant, interchangeable,
but are distinctive, as unique as snowflakes

or fingerprints, individuality only possible
to see up close, if you pay attention,
if you understand why it's important
to recognize the differences at all.

Fiction

Sara Sha

Mary Sees *Mona Lisa* and Changes her Life

As Mary watched the full moon's reflection ripple on the Seine, she tried to come to terms with her bitter disappointment.

While there was never anyone who encouraged her outright, there were always videos and songs and memes that told her, begged her, nagged her to pursue her dream. And her dream took root in art class her senior year.

She'd been mercifully ignored through high school. She did average work, so teachers neither praised her nor hovered over her desk in consternation. She was an average waitress, so customers neither left huge tips nor complained about her to the manager. She didn't even leave an impression at home where her father fell asleep in front of the television each night.

She felt safe in what she considered an average life: pass classes in school, read a book from time to time, get adequate sleep.

But then there was the *Mona Lisa*. The annoying *Mona Lisa*.

Look at the Mona Lisa, her art teacher crooned. *Look at her mysterious smile; what is she thinking? This painting has enchanted generations, tickled imaginations, brought people to their knees. This painting has inspired songs, stories, other painters. Look at her,* sigh, *just look at her.*

Mary looked at her. And felt nothing. Nothing at all.

Mary was used to feeling nothing at all, but this time it made her uneasy. She was able to cry at sad movies, laugh at videos, feel excitement from a good song. These were all reality checks for her; if she could feel the things she was expected to feel, then she was okay, she was normal, she could go on living her quiet, placid life.

But the *Mona Lisa*.

She looked around at her classmates and they had expressions of intrigue, or at least interest. No one was conveying confusion or disinterest or what-the-fuck-is-the-big-deal.

She looked up at the screen again and figured it must be due to some subtle pixelation. This wasn't the actual *Mona Lisa*, of course, just a photo. Maybe it was something that needed to be seen in person.

And right then, average, quiet, unseen Mary decided she would do just that. She would go to Paris.

While her senior classmates were planning their graduation parties and preparing for college, Mary was getting her passport and booking her hotel and making a budget. While her classmates were signing yearbooks and laughing over memories, Mary was learning phrases of useful language and metro schedules. While her classmates waved good-bye to their parents and left for opportunities in bigger cities, Mary quietly kissed her sleeping father's cheek and slipped out the door to the taxi waiting outside, leaving a note of explanation propped up on the coffee pot on the kitchen counter.

Mary marveled at her meticulous planning, but missed one detail. The crowd. She didn't consider that after plunking down her budgeted francs for admission, she would be one of tens of people jostling for position to view the painting. After catching a glimpse of the *Mona Lisa* before a large man maneuvered in front of her, she gave up her spot and went and sat on a bench not far from the crowd. She figured at some point the people would thin out and she could stand square in front of the painting and encourage it to fill her with passion and awe.

But the people kept coming. Sometimes a voice in the crowd would let out a shout from a crushed toe or an elbow in the eye, and Mary grew tired, tired from the planning, the plane trip, the change in time zones. As the afternoon wore on, she wandered through the endless halls of the Louvre and found pieces that captured her interest, but she always headed back to the *Mona Lisa* and was disappointed when the crowd was bigger than it was when she left.

She reflected on her folly as she watched a tour boat go by, this expensive trip, this sopping, saturating disappointment. She turned and looked up at the moon and thought of the times she'd looked up at it from her own bedroom window, an ocean away from everything that was familiar.

And then she felt marvel sneak in as she saw the lights of the Eiffel Tower in the distance and realized she was in actual Paris, France. She felt the cobblestones under her feet, she smelled the smoky, sweet air. She let in the immenseness of her accomplishment of leaving her white bread hometown to stand right here in one of the most beautiful cities in the world.

She looked over the railing at the blackened Seine and let her disappointment slide off into its inky depths. Tomorrow morning she would get up early and explore. She would have a croissant at a sidewalk cafe, she would take photographs of the Eiffel Tower from every angle.

She would let herself open up and spread herself all over this city, her heart pumping passion and fascination through her and outside of her, making her one with the museums and castles and countryside of this amazing place.

She might be average, quiet, unseen Mary, but no longer was it to avoid life, because now she would create her own wonderful secrets built on exotic experiences. And as she walked past the boisterous nighttime crowds in the bistros, she tried on her own mysterious smile.

Poetry
Charmaine Pappas Donovan

Ghost Sister
You are an apparition flimsy as fog,
elusive as the subtle smell of woodsmoke
out of sight, beyond my reach.

Once we lived in the same room,
battled over our side of *everything*—
especially that sway-back double bed.

We kicked each other in the shins,
yelled, beat one another bloody,
played hopscotch, war, ball & jacks.

Now you live across town, I'm told.
Your voice still echoes back to me.
Do you catch the sound of me in you?

Words logjam and fall through.
A closeness we held fell like leaves
along the paths we spent apart.

Our sad and silly trails split.
I never drank again. You chose the party life.
Had I not left it for good, I would be dead.

I will go to my grave, ghost sister,
visiting haunts where we once stood together
close enough to breathe each other's air.

Fiction
Niomi Rohn Phillips

When the Bough Breaks

Rosemary had never indulged in mining the details of winter 1950, "wallowing in it," her grandmother would have said. In fact, she'd worked at forgetting, but now, on the brink of old age, the sadness of remembering shadowed every day, and the flashes of fury frightened her.

"Panic attacks," Dr. Sylar called the pounding heart and sweating flushes. Not an impending heart attack, more likely "unresolved grief."

"What's happening in your family?" Sylar asked. "We suppress traumatic things and move on, but a significant event brings it back . . . Your granddaughter's high school graduation? Maybe you *have to go back* to resolve it."

So here she was driving across the prairie from one end of North Dakota to the other on her way to the Sisters of Mercy Home for Unwed Mothers, mentally unearthing details she'd spent a lifetime burying: the gray-green ceiling of the delivery room, her legs trapped in stirrups, the chapel where Sister Magdalena passed the babies to adopting parents.

She finally saw the Fargo exit signs, remembered The Home was near the river, and drove the tree-lined streets. The concrete pillars at the entrance to the curving driveway were there, but the "Sisters of Mercy" plaque was gone. The house wasn't as impressive—or intimidating—as the place in her memory.

She stopped at the edge of the driveway inside the pillars and put one hand over the other to stop the shaking. Then she put her head on the steering wheel and wept—for her seventeen-year-old self and the baby boy she gave away.

"Forget this. Go on with your life," the nuns told the girls who "got themselves in trouble." And she had.

She backed out of the driveway and retreated—to the big box world and the Ramada Inn. Past and future warred in her all night. What if granddaughter Sarah, a freshman at Carleton College, knew? No one Sarah's age would understand. Nowadays girls kept their babies. They weren't afraid of shaming their families.

Even her daughters wouldn't understand. She could hear them: "You just gave your baby away? We have a brother you never told us about?"

And Steve . . . "I've deceived you for over forty years."

"Some people can leave the scab over the wound," Dr. Sylar had said. "For now . . . you might want to know what records are available."

She waited for the County Court House to open the next morning, rehearsing her questions, then heard her own meek request to the Records Clerk, "I am wondering if birth records are open?"

"No, but you can look at an indexed list of births. Are you doing genealogy?"

"No . . . No . . . just a personal thing. I'm interested in a child born in 1950."

"You'll have to search for the date." The clerk plunked the 1950 volume on the table.

Rosemary's hands shook—handwritten lists, seven pages for December 12, 1950. She ran her finger down the columns looking for boys' names.

"The adoptive parents will name the baby," Sister Magdalena said. But when Rosemary held him, she thought about that spring afternoon with the meadowlarks singing, and she named him Daniel.

No Daniel. She closed the book. "Can you tell me what information would be on the birth certificate?"

"Child's name, mother's name including maiden name, father's name."

"What about adopted babies?" Rosemary asked.

"The adoptive parents' names. We replace the original record and mark it 'sealed.' It's in the State Records Bureau."

"What would I have to do to see the original?"

"Do you have the name?"

172

"No. No. I don't have a name . . . If a child is adopted, isn't there any way to find him?"

"What information *do* you have?"

"Only the date of birth."

"You'll have to write a letter to the County Judge. Ask for a court search. I don't do a thing without a signed order from the judge."

"I thought adoption records were open now."

"Adoptions may be open, but the record is still confidential."

Rosemary didn't know what she had expected. She had eleven names. She could track down eleven boys born on December 12, 1950, to find a forty-five-year-old man who might be adopted— and didn't know or didn't want to know.

Discouraged, drained, she realized she had to switch gears. Thanksgiving was a week away. She'd face it after Thanksgiving.

It was a good holiday—daughters, sons-in-law, grandkids together at daughter Carol's. Happy to have been with them, content in the quiet of the car on their way home, Steve and Rosemary slipped into their usual post-family-together review.

"The sun is always shining in Sarah's corner," Steve said.

"She's lucky. Girls have a lot of freedom these days."

"We've been pretty lucky, Rosemary." He reached for her hand and held it between them on the console.

Rosemary dozed. The hum of the car lulled her into the sleep she couldn't get at night when her brain fed the knots in her stomach. The steady rain helped. The car swerved. She startled awake. Ice. Steve struggled for control.

Dr. Sylar recognized the names on the evening news:

Freezing rain was responsible for six highway deaths this holiday weekend. Steve Hauser and his wife Rosemary were returning to Minot from Minneapolis . . . He was pronounced dead at the scene.

Poetry
Mary Willette Hughes

Last Night, a Fierce Ice Storm
Morning comes. Outside, dawn glows in pulsing
    rosy hues and night's sun-sheathed leaves glisten.
Our basswood tree, decorated with fall's clinging
    golden colors, whispers: *stand still, hush yourself.*

I listen intently and hear the smallest, the tiniest
    tinkling sounds as ice-encased leaves move gently
against each other, creating a delicate pilgrim music;
    it journeys from my inner ear to my amazed heart.

Creative Nonfiction
Mike Lein

A Change In Power

I was out on the cold ice of Cracked Lake when it dawned on me that the times, they are a-changing. I had just punched five or six holes through the ice, searching for the elusive silver-sided crappies that swim beneath. This chore had been accomplished with minimal effort through the use of my brand new battery-powered ice auger. I was cleaning out the holes when Cabin Neighbor Tom pulled up on his four-wheeler with his green and black electric auger mounted on the front.

"Nice auger! How many volts is that thing?" he asked.

I swelled up a little with pride and gave him the facts—"It says 120 volts right on it!"

I could tell Tom had a bad case of power envy. "Damn," he said. "Mine's only twenty-four."

Take notice, all you hearty Northwoods guys and gals. Change is acomin'! We have measured our power and worth in the North Country in amounts soon to be outdated. Well-known measures such as horsepower are about to become as obsolete and as useless as a horse at the Indy 500. Gasoline-powered machines and tools, the very ones we use to turn trees into firewood, to get to the other side of the lake, or to rumble through the snow of winter and the mud of spring, will soon be rusting in junkyards.

More importantly, with this transformation will come the need to find new ways of measuring our power and thus our prestige in our local communities. Few of us are true physicists who fully comprehend the formulas used to calculate things like "horsepower." I will admit that I gotta "D" in the one Physics class required back in college and was happy to move on with it. But we do understand that 350 horsepower is a lot for a truck and that 150 horsepower isn't. And furthermore, we understand that the more horsepower you have, the more power and prestige you have with what some people would call "our peers."

Forget about that electric ice auger. Some electric cars are now quicker and faster and more powerful than those old muscle cars we used to lust over as teenagers. I've been reading reports that heavy-duty electric trucks are almost among us. Ones that will effortlessly haul boats, campers, and big loads of firewood.

The question is not whether this will happen. Those forces are in motion and beyond our control. The real question is how we will adapt to these changes. How will we now measure our power and therefore our worth so that we clearly understand who is leading the race of Life? Who is "The Man" or "The Woman"? Perhaps we even need to change that terminology to "The Person."

I suggest we take one thing at a time and establish our power-measuring system first. Based on my limited knowledge, just counting volts like Tom was doing, doesn't cut it. We all know the cheap 20-volt cordless drill us cabin owners buy in a discount store, doesn't have the durability and power of the 20-volt drill our contractor uses to fix the mistakes we created with ours. There has to be more to the story. Something maybe to do with watts, since we all know the 100-watt bulb flooding the yard with light burns brighter than the 40-watt bulb in the basement.

There's even a less understood, at least by me, thing called an "amp." So help me out here. Think about this and be ready for a serious discussion of power around the next neighborhood campfire. I imagine this is going to boil down to some damn formula like volts divided by watts multiplied by the square of pi over amps. And that scares me for our future. I'll never know how I stack up against my neighbors. 'Cause I never was very good at math either.

Poetry
Jennifer Hernandez

On the Occasion of my Child's Commencement
I wish for you the breath
to blow the fluff of a dandelion,
the candles of a birthday cake,
a kiss. For a loved one
to catch that kiss—this time
a mother, who watches proudly
just out of focus, not wanting
attention, only the relief
of knowing that she did enough,
that you can take it from here,
feet on solid ground,
body healthy and strong,
clothed in bright confident colors
as you step into the sunshine,
from the shadow of home
into the wide open field,
long wild grasses dancing,
mountains stretching out in front.
Knowing that life can be as fragile
as the filaments your breath has loosed,
as subject to chance as the vagaries
of the breeze. You might parachute
to the ground here at my feet
or float away on a warm current.

Poetry
Susan Niemela Vollmer

Mind Travel
Each month   each season
my mind carries me back to where I traveled
in years past at this same time

Autumn brings the rides on rustic winding roads
driving a daughter to Michigan's Upper Peninsula
or other trips through convoluted city routes
to the University of Minnesota
after the disastrous bridge collapse

October gusts carry a sadness
that reminds me of my father's funeral
emotion doesn't acknowledge
that almost forty years have passed

Today I travel to pre-pandemic times
the hills and curves convey us
past broad cornfields and faded barns
restlessly counting the miles
between our grandchildren and our arms

"The talking stick is a Native American tradition used to facilitate an orderly discussion. The stick is made of wood, decorated with feathers or fur, beads or paint, or a combination of all. Usually speakers are arranged in a talking circle and the stick is passed from hand to hand as the discussion progresses. It encourages all to speak and allows each person to speak without interruption. The talking stick brings all natural elements together to guide and direct the talking circle." —Anne Dunn

This year, we received nearly 350 submissions from 158 writers. From these, the Editorial Board selected 91 poems, 24 creative nonfiction stories, and 16 fiction from 100 writers for inclusion in this volume.

Please submit again!

www.thetalkingstick.com
www.jackpinewriters.com

Without the following contributors in 2020, this Talking Stick would not have been possible. Thank you to everyone!

Benefactors
Larry Ellingson
Mike and Marlys Guimaraes
Dawn Loeffler
Richard and Carol Sederstrom
Harlan and Marlene Stoehr
Steven and Mary Vogel

Special Friends
Sue Bruns
Sharon Chmielarz
Mike Lein
Linda Maki
Susan McMillan
Kathleen Pettit
Niomi Rohn Phillips
Elizabeth Weir

Good Friends
Tim Brennan
Crow Wing Crest
Frances Crowley

Jennifer Fackler
Cindy Fox
Dan McKay
Vincent O'Connor
Ron Palmer
Polly Scotland
LeRoy Sorenson
Doris Stengel

Friends
Michelle Blenkush
Sarah Cox
Colleen Gengler
Marilyn groenke
JJ Harrigan
Marcus Kessler
Victoria Smith
Anne Stewart
Joanna Swanson
Bernadette Thomasy
Peggy Trojan

T. S. Baxter
Lina Belar
Rani Bhattacharyya
Kate Bitters
Micki Blenkush
212 Jim Bohen
Nicole Borg
Jana Bouma
Kim M. Bowen
Mary Lou Brandvik
Janice Larson Braun
Tim J. Brennan
Sue Bruns
Marc Burgett
Sharon Chmielarz
Jan Chronister
Mary A.Conrad
Susan Coultrap-McQuin
Joanne Cress
Frances Ann Crowley
Norita Dittberner-Jax
Charmaine Pappas Donovan
Phyllis Emmel
Jeanne Emrich
Jeanne Everhart
Edis Flowerday
Marsha Foss
Cindy Fox
Katie Gilbertson
Georgia A. Greeley
Matt Gregersen
Marlys Guimaraes
Tara Flaherty Guy
Ramae Hamrin
Laura L. Hansen
Paula Hari
Sharon Harris
Mary Fran Heitzman
Audrey Kletscher Helbling
Lane Henson
Jennifer Hernandez
Mary Willette Hughes
Donna Isaac
Anne M. Jackson
Jennifer Jesseph
Christina Joyce
Teri Joyce
Amanda Valerie Judd
Sandra Kacher
Meridel Kahl

Charles Kausalik-Boe
Kathryn Knudson
M. E. Kopp
Laura Krueger-Kochmann
Kristin Laurel
Mike Lein
Doug Lewandowski
Dawn Loeffler
Linda Maki
Christine Marcotte
Erin Marsh
Susan McMillan
Liz Minette
Christopher Mueller
Marsh Muirhead
Ryan M. Neely
L. E. Newsom
Joni Norby
Vincent O'Connor
Yvonne Pearson
Darrell J. Pedersen
Kathleen J. Pettit
Niomi Rohn Phillips
Adrian Potter
Deborah Rasmussen
Amy C. Rea
Kit Rohrbach
Mary Kay Rummel
Stephanie Sanderson
Deb Schlueter
Ruth M. Schmidt-Baeumler
Richard Fenton Sederstrom
Anne Seltz
Sara Sha
Victoria Lynn Smith
Anne Stewart
Marlene Mattila Stoehr
Bernadette Hondl Thomasy
Peggy Trojan
Lucy Tyrrell
Donna Uphus
Joel Van Valin
Steven R. Vogel
Beth L. Voigt
Susan Niemela Vollmer
Ben Westlie
Mary Scully Whitaker
Pam Whitfield
Cheryl Weibye Wilke
Pamela Wolters